11/16

D1564611

THE BRIG

THE BRIG

A Concept for Theatre or Film by
KENNETH H. BROWN

With an Essay on The Living Theatre *by*
JULIAN BECK

and Director's Notes by
JUDITH MALINA

•

A Spotlight Dramabook
HILL AND WANG · NEW YORK

FIRST EDITION MARCH 1965
SECOND PRINTING OCTOBER 1967
THIRD PRINTING JUNE 1968
FOURTH PRINTING FEBRUARY 1969

A longer version of *The Brig* was published in the *Tulane Drama Review* (Spring, 1964). The text printed here is the acting script used in The Living Theatre production.

Manufactured in the United States of America by
The Colonial Press Inc., Clinton, Massachusetts

MISTER BECK WITHOUT REEFER

THE VERSION of Storming The Barricades printed in this edition is Mister Beck in clean clothes, Mister Beck as gentleman, Mister Beck without reefer.

The publisher chose to make over 600 alterations in the text without my knowledge or permission, verbal or contractual.

I am an anarchist. I dont sue, I dont get injunctions, I advocate revolution, and when people ask me what can we do that's practical, I say, weakly, weaken the fabric of the system wherever you can, make possible the increase of freedom, all kinds. When I write I try to extend the possibilities of expression.

Saw the final proofs here in jail a week ago, despite publisher's reluctance to send them. I had tried to speak to you honestly, my own way, undisguised, trying to get rid, it's part of my obligation to the muse, of the ancien regime of grammar.

So the version that appears here has been given the copyeditor college theme treatment. Hardly a word has been changed tho, must make that clear, a couple of cuts, o.k. except for one, but the revisions in typography and punctuation have taken from the voice the difference that distinguishes passion from affection and me speaking to you from me writing an essay.

I look at it now and have a little the feeling I might have if the barbed wire that separates the audience from the action in The Brig had been removed, because somebody thought the spectators could see better that way. The publisher told my mother he had had the manuscript changed to make it easier for the reader. Easier to understand me if I'm dressed as conformist. You know that isnt my way. And that I dont condescend.

A few errata. We were at The Cherry Lane from December 1951 to August 1952, at 100th Street from March 1954 to

November 1955, at 14th Street from January 1959 to October 1963. The 4 paragraphs describing how we did The Marrying Maiden were written by Judith. And in the 7th paragraph from the end there's a reference to prison noise that once killed applause. That's about the opening of Many Loves when I had a conscious encounter with the uncanny, as I stood on the stage the sound of the applause was drowned out by the memory of the noise in the corridors of the Tombs.

At first this whole episode threw me into despair. If the publisher of The Brig didnt know what I was trying to do, if he had a higher opinion of convention than of the artist's intention to keep literature free, then what to expect from the less enlightened man.

But that is why I put more faith in the people, who, despite fearful ignorance and prejudice, have the least to lose when the revolution comes.

There's a lot of work to do.

The publisher made it clear he was going to print the piece as he wanted no matter what. Yesterday, thru the intervention of Judith, he offered to print verbatim anything I wanted to say by way of explanation. Here it is.

Havent succeeded in squelching my spite as I write this, nor in writing this beyond my vanity. That's part of the work. Literary fights always look funny five years later. So will this.

JULIAN BECK

Danbury Prison
January 18, 1965

CONTENTS

	page
Mister Beck Without Reefer by Julian Beck	v
Storming the Barricades by Julian Beck	1
Productions of The Living Theatre	37
The Brig by Kenneth H. Brown	39
Directing *The Brig* by Judith Malina	108

STORMING THE BARRICADES

STORMING THE BARRICADES

A PLAY ARRIVES in the mail. I open it at random and read a line. If the line is good, I go on, maybe start from the beginning and read the whole thing. I will not submit myself to reading a play if the writing is not good. And for the same reason will not submit any audience to it. Who am I to judge? And in this hard and arrogant way. "I am but an erring mortal," writes Gandhi, progressing from blunder toward truth. And I, may my blunders not cause pain, not to playwrights, not to anyone, and, as for truth, may we all get there.

The work of any important playwright. Open at random. Ibsen, Marlowe, Strindberg, Cocteau. The language is always good, like light. Language is the key. It opens the doors that keep us locked in confining chambers, the Holy of Holies, the instrument of unification, communication, and from communication let us derive the word community. The community is love, impossible without it, and the syllogism affirms then that love, as we humans may supremely create it, rises and falls with language. Yes, the grunts of animals in the act of coitus—music for the ears of heaven. The proper sounds, the stresses, the silences, the grunts that rise from real feeling, satisfaction with food or with your body as I animally caress it; those sounds wrenched from my groin upward and out of the throat, they please you, because they are honest and near to God.

To see the human face, to hear the spoken word, the two maxima of experience. Eric Gutkind. But this is not easy. Not the face of corruption, not the abstracted face of the servile citizen of the abstract state, not the face grown expressionless through the fear of the dicta of a scared society, not the face that does not represent the climax of physical being, not the face that is a mask—mask of virtue, mask of preference, mask of distortion, falsehood, and failure—but the face the sight of which makes creation that much easier. And the spoken word must be the word we use when I speak to thee, not the language of deception, not the misuse of the word in order to dissemble, language that ultimately separates. The word must join us, else it is just another barricade. We kill one another when we do not speak the truth; it is the way to early death. But when you speak to me true I live, and you live a little longer. It is our joint struggle against death. The prolongation of this life depends on exaltation through exalted speech. Speech: the poet reading aloud, the actor speaking the word, not on the page, but in the ear. And that is why we crown with laurel those heroes who have strained to bring us knowledge of language that vaults the degradations of the unloving ways of the world: Aeschylus, the Prophets, Lao-tse, Rilke, Shelley, Joyce, Dante, the lovers under the quilts, and the fine practical language of woodsmen building a bridge, another plank. The miracle happens when speech unites.

The Brig arrived in the mail. I opened it. Knew instantly that it was the next play we would do. Read it that night. It was as if everything in my life had led to the occasion. How?

I come from a middle-class background, Jewish. There is a brilliant connection, like a hideous fluorescent tunnel, that leads from Washington Heights, where I was born and grew up and educated, to putting *The Brig* on a stage. *The Brig*, 1963, the consummation of my life in the theatre.

Washington Heights, legal trickery, spiritual debasement and the systematic indoctrination of the servile spirit, which process is known as education. Emma Goldman. Thus, that night, reading *The Brig*, at home, Garry Beck, thirteen, 1:30 A.M., is sweating over a theme for English, a thousand words, fatigued, the words painful, not the words of unification, but forced, resented, ached out, must be completed no matter how late, how tired, lest he have to write a two thousand word theme. To punish with language. Sir, Prisoner Number One requests permission to cross the white line.

When I asked William Carlos Williams what *Many Loves* was about, he said it was about accuracies. *The Brig* was fulfilling the promise made by Williams. He got accuracies fully in his poems and many times in *Many Loves,* but Brown, panting, never stops, accuracy after accuracy with no blank space in between, and there, documented, were all the crimes of abstract feelingless authoritarianism. A play in which the two dim moments of real speech, "Did you get to Tokyo last night?" and "We had a ball in Tokyo last night," are thrilling even in their feebleness. They speak to us from the abode where the immortals are. It is speech, no matter how stuck in the throat, it is the blessed speech that communicates friendliness, and if there were more of it, so softly spoken and rising from the warmer regions of the body, enough of it to displace the rest of the language of the play, all the sentences that begin with "Sir," why then we could get off this arid plateau, to the next, where the problems of life will be less deranging and still more beautiful.

After Washington Heights and the RKO on Saturdays, school plays, report cards, and the leg irons of all the social mores, adolescence, pining for sophistication, and the scent of art tempting me to keep going. I am talking about *The Brig* and the elements that went into its production. At the age of sixteen, with Geminitic alacrity, I changed from seeking conservative refinement and accomplishment to courting the flaming bride, incandescent, revolution. Always strewn with humanistic, "istic" meaning sort of, notions, it's the life of art, I'm seventeen, writing, painting, planning work in the theatre, but always with a friend. I don't like to work alone, I adore collaboration, to join with someone and to do something; much more gratifying than working alone, because something else is happening; it's very sexy, even when you are not really fucking; you are filling someone else, and someone else is filling or is filled by you. Not a substitution for the McCoy, but something else, and full of its own aromas.

Judith. No secret that our commitment to the theatre

is not exclusive. Is this connected with unification? I don't know. I suspect so, but I am uncertain.

Judith. If I am a compass, she is North.

The Living Theatre is forming itself; may it always be forming itself and never finally formed, stonelike, irrevocable, resistant to motion, heavy, irresponsive, a graven image, unable to comprehend the living God.

This was not always so. You start out to build a temple, you end by gathering sticks for a hut. 1946–47. Starting out to build a temple. Elaborate plans. Architectural designs. Loyalty to art. Juvenile concepts because we were juveniles. To make a theatre combining real music, dance, painting, and poetry. In fact, our first statement said something about encouraging the poets to write for the theatre by providing them with a stage where their plays could be produced. The first impulse, therefore a revulsion, against sham. The poetry we wanted had not yet been written and still has not been written. The stage is still there.

There has been some theatre verse in the last twenty years that I respect, but not enough, and still too dependent on the verse spirit of other eras to speak directly, engagingly, to the audiences of our time. We wait and work, because when it happens it will happen because we are prepared for it. By "we" I mean everyone, not only needing it, but wanting it, craving it, because we want to take flight—poetry after all is flight—and then we will be flying, man, then, not now, beyond even yearning, but ready to take poetic action, that's when.

But we did start off by doing Lorca, Goodman, Rexroth, Stein, Eliot, Auden, and William Carlos Williams, or plays in which the language was that kind of prose which makes the unconscious telegraphic leaps that poets are masters of —Strindberg, Cocteau, Picasso, Ashbery, Brecht, Jarry. Interesting that The Living Theatre's climactic work, *The Connection* and *The Brig*, was in the scrutiny of actuality. "Poetry of the theatre," says Cocteau, not meaning meter; the phrase turned on the line, that kind of thing, but something else, which in the work of Brown and Gelber emerges as the distillation, extraction, representation of exact words and action of life as it is lived, honest, uncompromisingly honest, and by being life itself and not sham is some kind of poetry, something which flies, uplifts, probably because being very near to life itself, we are moved, as we are moved by poetry, because it is close to life, shows us life itself, and that is always the only encouraging thing. That is, nothing exceeds life itself, the human face, the spoken word, but it has then to be itself, not armor instead of flesh, not lies instead of speech. In Brown and Gelber then is an intimation of poetry more elevated and profound, frail though it is, a blueprint on tissue paper, but nearer to truth, which poetry always is, than all the oratory everywhere, off stage and on, of our time. Something like that.

Our initial commitment was with form. That was why the first play we did at our first Cherry Lane season, 1951, was by Gertrude Stein. The work of Stein was attractive to us because it never ceased being part of the revolution of the word, a period in international literature of the first couple of decades of this century which tried to revivify language, which did revivify language, and with it the structure, the form, of literature, by erasing the platitudes and exploring and pushing at the boundaries of meaning in writing. How can you have a lively civilization if the language is outmoded and no longer says what anyone can possibly want to mean? How can you enlarge the limits of consciousness if language atrophies? How can you approach real conscious being if the language is just hanging around? The difference between mere conscious being and true existence is the nearness to God. Buber. Relentlessly, Stein worked with form in an attempt to surface sunken knowledge, not simply information, but the light-shedding qualities of metaphysical and psychological associations, and, what is perhaps more, exactness. To find out what is really there, to examine everything, common objects, and to define them, not partially, but totally and exactly, so that when we see and think,

we see what is really there, and when we think, we think
thoroughly. This was her experiment. It did not stop with
prose description but carried on into varied forms of literature, not the least of which, in this woman's prolific output,
was in theatre. She wrote over forty plays and librettos. There
is an impression that she tried to drive narrative out of the
theatre, but if she did attempt this I do not think she
succeeded. Something is always happening in her work, and
she relied on the director, or scenarist, to freely supply the
action suggested by the words and the rhythms and divisions
of the dialogue. We wanted to do some of her work and
wanted to open The Living Theatre with *Doctor Faustus
Lights the Lights* because it was like a manifesto and would
always stand at the head of our work saying take the clue
from this.

    Doctor Faustus Lights the Lights and *The Brig* are like
mirrors locked face to face. But one mirror is taller than the
other. I'm sure of that. One of them is wider, but I'm not
sure of that. Both do minimize the narrative. Both are concerned with examining minutely a moral sensibility and
both are concerned with identity. Both are deeply formed
by the rhythms they create. Both are involved with electric
light. In his opening stage directions Brown says that the
stage is suddenly bathed in light: white, bright, and electric.
The entire action is subjected to this light; the light is an
integral part of the stage production, just as the light is an
integral part of *Doctor Faustus*. I should mention the light
bulb that hangs in the center of the stage of *The Connection*.
The Stein play pivots on the question of how to get to Hell.
Mephisto advises Faustus to kill anything. This question is
never asked in *The Brig*, but unannounced it is there all the
time. *The Brig* itself is a kind of Hell. You don't have to
ask. It is not a theoretical Hell, not imaginary, not theo-
logical, above all not that; it is the Hell which is the judg-
ment of man, it is the Hell of everything that puts people
in cages and that draws rigid lines. So the work of Stein and
the play of Brown, our first major production and our last,

to date, are quite close. There is one great difference. The Stein play is, like most international theatre of the last hundred years, offered to the intellect, the theatre of the intellect, sometimes called the Theatre of Ideas, and Brown's play is that, too, but something else has been added. Brown's play is kinetic, and though there is no grand ballet—Stein calls for one in her play—*The Brig* is visual, and it is intended not only to affect the mind but to affect the viscera. It is the torment of Artaud; it is the Theatre of Cruelty, this *Brig*; it is unbearable rather than compatible; it is horror rather than beauty; it is hysterical rather than reasonable. It aims to undo you rather than compose you. *Doctor Faustus Lights the Lights* appeals to you, emphasis on the word appeals, appeals. *The Brig* assaults. Total assault on the culture. Ed Sanders.

Now this growth from *Doctor Faustus* to *The Brig* can be regarded, with the usual vagueness with which we regard things, as a development. What is the difference between development and change? I call for change all the time nowadays. That's what I reach for in these dark times as we all face annihilation, if not by bomb on the body then by clamp on the brain or by the fences of restriction that keep us from touching one another. As intellectual theatre *The Brig* is no more exemplary than *Doctor Faustus*; as upheaval theatre it is.

We announced the first season at the Cherry Lane with three plays. In addition to the Stein play, we listed Kenneth Rexroth's *Beyond the Mountains* and Paul Goodman's *Faustina*. Both plays are in verse. That was only the beginning of the verse plays. In the course of the years, we did *Sweeney Agonistes, The Age of Anxiety, The Idiot King, Phèdre, The Cave at Machpelah, Women of Trachis,* and in "part-time verse," that is, plays with some scenes in verse and some in prose, *Many Loves, The Young Disciple, Man Is Man.* We had our greatest difficulties with verse plays. All kinds of agony. Sometimes they worked, especially the part-time ones. The greater number account for our most renowned failures. Interesting statistic that except for *Sweeney*, which was on a triple bill including the Picasso play and Stein's *Ladies' Voices*, the opening nights of the verse plays were all postponed. Postponement is a nightmare sequence. Nobody wants to. The cast is reluctant because it means the recognition of the fact that the work, the actors' work, has not been going well. Usually everything is not going well: the production is always behind time, it costs more. The critics and public know that it usually means trouble. You can never tell the truth, that is, you never send out a release saying more time is needed to rehearse this play, you never send out a release saying we haven't solved all the problems; you always have to dissemble and make believe it's a casting affair, a technical impediment, an illness, a conflict with another company's opening; you pray, as it is said, for a coincidence to provide an excuse, and it means prolonging the anguish. Maybe verse plays, like spectacles, need more rehearsal time. May be as simple as that and probably is, probably because we do not have at our disposal a natural affinity to verse and a great deal of the time during rehearsal is expended on discovering a satisfactory style for the production. We rarely found this style. Always our tendency to blame ourselves and not the playwright. If the play doesn't work it is because we have not found the means of making it work. Cast often disagrees. Conflict, yes, unpleasantness, dissension, and then the bad business of the company losing faith in the directors and the directors despairing of the company. All this is surface.

All this is surface. What is really happening in these verse plays? I can't get away with saying that Auden, Brecht, Pound, Sophocles, Goodman, and Rexroth aren't good playwrights or that these plays are merely not their best work. Cheesy cop-out, confining their efforts to the closet and so forth. Major writers, after all, and whatever they might do in the theatre bound to be interesting, and their theatrical instincts worth plenty of attention. It is the function of a theatre such as The Living Theatre to do their works. No, the duty. The responsibility. What is the failure, and where?

Instant answer: we don't know how to do them right. The actors don't know how to speak the verse, make it come alive, nor the directors, nor do we know how to make glow the formal structures and theatrical devices of the theatre of verse, that is, a formal theatre, a theatre not of the realist style; how to make it into I don't know what. Having trouble finding the right word for what they should be made into. All I come up with are negatives like not into something creepy, not into something phony, pompous, not into something arty, pretentious, not into something disjointed, a series of effects, a vehicle for aural or pictorial effects. Bad. But I don't let the poet-playwrights completely off the hook. That's what I meant when I said I was not altogether satisfied with the theatre verse of our time. The poets need to find a way to make their language hit the mark, and the mark is you and me. These are all clues to the problem, or at least to the problems we have with such plays. I am quick to state that I have never attended verse theatre anywhere done to my satisfaction. I would be satisfied by any verse theatre that aroused my better, not my baser, instincts.

What are these baser instincts? Fake notions of grandeur, bullshit beauty, intoxication with wigs instead of hair. Fetishes, when my sexual instincts are aroused by clothing instead of bodies, my mind by superimposed symbol glamour, legless ideas, bodiless creation. Simple arithmetic—the problem is to get closer to life. Paradox: nothing in the theatre can get closer to life than verse and nothing further away, nothing further away as when the verse strays into representing that kind of life which never ought to be.

At the beginning, in *Beyond the Mountains* and *Faustina*, we tried to bring formal elements into the theatre, counterattack on the prevalent theatre which knew only that Yeats wasn't good box office. But what to do with this verse, this vaulting language, the piercing phrases which illuminate your life forever, the whole staggering jumble of harmony of all things poetry, yet which when divorced from the body, from movement, from action, from the confrontation which means this life here and now as well as all those other plateaus on which we are conscious and unconscious, becomes like dead tissue, the severed head of a beautiful woman, disgusting?

How to attach the head to the body? How to make this verse into a living thing? We don't know what to do with the verse and the poets aren't giving us theatre verse suited to our powers. It goes back and forth. Together is what I am saying, collaborate, in community, to find the answer.

Time as always to ask questions. The degree of our confusion and failure in this area of theatre is apparent, right now, as I write about it. I do not have the answers for the failure, not for mine, nor for other directors. But the questions are there to be asked, and asked again and again until we crack the code, code of verse, code of Aeschylus, of Racine, of Shakespeare, of Yeats, of Rexroth, Goodman, Pound. How do we find out what the plays mean and how do we communicate that meaning, how do we make what happens to us in the library happen on the stage more forcefully—by "we" I mean actors and poets—more gloriously, more excellently well? How do we learn to write a language, speak that language, express and enact that passion, vault those concepts? Is there something missing in those plays? Is there something missing in ourselves? Is there something wrong with them, with us, with everything? Must you wait until one has the answers before working with these plays? Must you wait until, alone, contemplating, meditating, the answer is arrived at? Is that possible? Can the answer be found only through trial and error? Who sets the values? Is there a right and a wrong about anything? Why is the actor playing Hamlet always more interesting nowadays than the play? Was it ever different? Will it ever be? Ought it to be? Are we wrong in our assumptions about verse? Is Aeschylus a deadhead, verse a romantic notion, a longing for things we ought not to long for? Who are these kings and princes?

Are their images sickening in themselves, doomed to decay, best buried, so they simply no longer speak to our time? Should we forget them, should we then thus cut off the past from our being? Are we the sum of civilization? Is the thesis of duty to eternity and to the lives that have been lived and the things men have created a false hypothesis? How can we leave these questions lying about discarded? What is the good of answers without the pleasure and the glory of the struggle in the seeking?

In *Beyond the Mountains* we used all kinds of artifice, masks, dances, as in the Noh plays, to express the inexpressible climaxes, sumptuous lighting, plain costumes, all black and white and golds, large squares of cloth tied with ropes; we spoke Rexroth's baroque verse clearly and attempted a kind of musical speech, perhaps too much Schumann and not enough Cage.

Goodman's *Faustina* had a symbolic set: hearts, livers, a cunt-couch, and a grand scenic effect in which the formal walling architecture, the civilization of Rome, disappeared and gave way to a free and empty stage devoid of all trappings—a moment of breakthrough into the present with a speech in which Faustina approached the audience and tried to make contact, saying, "We have enacted a brutal scene, the ritual murder of a young and handsome man. I have bathed in his blood, and if you were a worthy audience, you'd have leaped on the stage and stopped the action." The audience was insulted and went away annoyed, riled by the affront. We spoke the verse Goodman had written simply this time, strong, hard, bold. No dice.

On to Auden's *The Age of Anxiety*. More successful. We did all we could: we rehearsed the play for over a year, the five of us, and tried to release the multiple meanings, searching for a style in speaking that would be at once simple and real and yet preserve the additive meanings in the verse, scalpel through to the heritage of the unconscious and the intimations of metaphysical speculations. We were complimented and the audience was apathetic.

Another try with a heavy play, *The Idiot King*, the work of Claude Fredericks, who tried to have us speak about fundamental things—those persistent problems, life and death, love and war, killing and God, faith and morality— and we drew a blank. Staged simply, the order of the play proceeding easily from step to step, easy to follow, and failure. *Phèdre*, Racine's great thing. *The Idiot King* we put into vague contemporary clothes; Racine we did *à la romaine*, seventeenth-century costumes, a very formal approach, on a stark white set, glistening with light, the light that Racine talks about all through the play. Someone said it looked like an abstract Japanese ballet. We worked on the scenes of concealed and bursting passions trying to get to the pith, the fuse, the switch of those blazing passions, tried to lift the blind, bare the feeling. Part way, maybe, but not far enough.

The poetry continues in Goodman's play *The Cave at Machpelah*, which we did in 1959, a kind of epic thing, the language and action gradually evolving from some kind of high Corneille speech in the first act into the easy flow of Goodman's *Empire City* manner in the last. We explored various acting styles and possibilities and came up with the shortest run The Living Theatre ever had, seven performances.

Tried again with Pound's version of *Women of Trachis*. Blame the translation, blame the play, blame the director, the designer, the actors, the composer, blame everything but not ourselves—that we haven't found a way to be equal to these plays and, in the context of defeat, content ourselves with the prose of writers whose names cannot be mentioned in this same paragraph.

Now the verse in Goodman's *The Young Disciple*, in William Carlos Williams' *Many Loves* and Brecht's *Man Is Man* was less problematic. Didn't make us fall on our faces, that is. The verse in these plays is more natural, as we like to say, easier on the tongue, nearer the language of daily speech, but defined with a difference, an elegance, an exactness and a subtlety that ordinary speech doesn't carry.

This we could take and this we could cope with. Eliot has found, too, in *The Cocktail Party*, that refined speech with important overtones, plain, clear, lucid, precise, is the most workable formal poetry for the theatre of this period in time. Does it simply mean we are not capable of the more involved uncompromising verse that comes trailing clouds of images? That may be. But why do we recoil?

Examining further. The language of Picasso's play *Desire Trapped by the Tail*—we did it in a clean and fragrant translation by Herma Briffault (we always worry all night for weeks, months, about translations)—is complex, rich, luxuriant, colorful, wild, surreal, free. Also very funny. Clues.

The complexity of its language was no hindrance to breaking through. Nor its exotic character, nor its illogical sentence structure, nor its extravagance of imagery. There was no separation; it did join, so did the oddities of Goodman's *Young Disciple*, and Cocteau's free associations. That is, I am beginning to believe, we in the twentieth century are more eager to jump into a free and peculiar present or future than into a noble past. Mayhap we have had too much of that mile-high regality, and all in the wrong context. If this is so, know that I regard it as a good. How to do it? We would like to wrestle with Brecht's *Antigone*, his adaptation of Hölderlin's lyric lines. Try, try again.

When in December 1951—after mounting *Beyond the Mountains* we had no more money—we decided to cancel the projected production of *Faustina* and to do a triple bill: *Desire, Sweeney,* and *Ladies' Voices.* We titled the whole thing "An Evening of Bohemian Theatre," which bugged many people, but thought that if the public wasn't ready for Stein, Eliot, and Picasso, then maybe we better give up right then and there. The production was successful. That kind of abstraction could reach people, make contact, and evoke joy, mystery, and considerable laughter. A good kind of laughter because it was at no one's expense.

Yet eight years later when we launched Jackson MacLow's *The Marrying Maiden* in a production not aiming to evoke

laughter but delicately, strangely, to loosen chords in the
unconscious, start things vibrating with calculated serious-
ness, uncover a bit those lurking things—how else find out
about them?—we had to accept public failure. The play was
deliberately perplexing. The audience was baffled and few
honored the intention. Add, though, that the play's form
was relatively unfamiliar; the element of Chance, Indeterminacy was its blood. But the public showed no enthusiasm.
We were disappointed and we believed somehow that had
we made the play funny it would have made it. Clue. Laughter. Chaplin. To produce a physical reaction, make the belly
shake, mix up the head and eyes with the ridiculous, cracks
in the ice and armor, something happening to them. The
verse tragedies which I've been talking about, with all their
gorgeous language and the rotund passions, all the seething
emotions, and the stark dramatic moments, caught, roped,
garlanded with what we consider the attributes of splendor
—don't pierce the shell. Real feeling is not touched, only
attitudes of feeling, the outside. Maybe it's the regality
problem, no identification; we're outside. Then we must
begin to concentrate on ways to get in there, or, just as good,
a means to open the dam and let the insides flow out. If
the experiments fail—Ehrlich permitted himself 605 failures
—we still will be asking the question, unless we have found
a form of theatre that makes poetry obsolete. I expect that
might happen, and Shakespeare would become obsolete.

Perhaps all that writing must be left behind, the printed
word, the library forgotten. Artaud. Then a theatre in which
language pours from the throats of the actors: the high art
of improvisation, when the actor is like a great hero, the
partner of God. A man's proper job and position, isn't it, to
create, make life on the stage, there in our presence, doing
whatever he is doing at maximum, like a great great lover,
the new poetry flowing from his being, marvelous energy,
a river in spring, fertilizing the banks? He is the actor I
dream of, and his is the theatre I would like to go to, one
worthy, as I have often said, of the life of each spectator.

There are three neat periods which contain the stage history of The Living Theatre. The first period was at the Cherry Lane (August 1951–August 1952), the second at the loft on One Hundredth Street (March 1954–June 1959), the third at Fourteenth Street and Sixth Avenue (July 1959–January 1964). At the Cherry Lane we made our initial statements. At One Hundredth Street we set out to develop our craft. On Fourteenth Street we tried to establish a theatrical institution which, by gathering together, could assemble the forces needed to begin to tunnel through. The work at the Cherry Lane and at One Hundredth Street was mostly preparation; through the work we were storing up energy; we made mistakes there; we always make mistakes and sometimes learn from them; we began to show and then to shed, dispose of, early notions of staging, moving from rigidity toward a certain fluidity.

Example. At the Cherry Lane we prepared plays by making rather careful directing books. That is, we worked on the staging of the play in advance, considering the movements actors would make, the interpretation of lines. We prepared the set designs, the music, the costume designs ahead of time. We used this mode of preparation less and less as our work progressed, and nowadays neither Judith nor I indulge in the Reinhardt *Regiebuch*. We study the play before rehearsals begin; we talk, mull, discuss, discard, talk some more. I no longer make any designs for a play until I have heard the actors read it, not once but many times. I prefer not to make the costume designs until I have watched the staging and watched the actors move. I don't like to impose concepts, but rather let the designs emerge from the play, be an integral part of the staging and the actors' creative work. The system is not foolproof. Still heaps of mistakes, but the whole method is possibly moving in the direction of a creative ensemble, community, rather than a binding together of faggots, separate sticks; better a growing tree of course, something like that.

The work at the Cherry Lane had an aristocratic concern

with the aesthetics of stagecraft. What do I mean by that? Consciously, at least, our concern was with refinement. I fear that the influence of the Museum of Modern Art was a little too predominant. Perhaps not so much the influence of its aesthetic as the attitude of its aesthetic. Attitudes are not real feelings or real ideas. Character front. Perhaps our aesthetic itself has not so much changed as the attitude. Now we know that art is a means of communicating, not an end. At that earlier time we were dominated chiefly by form, line, color. You can only believe in them alone if you are attitudinizing. Chiefly.

There were other things, too; I am being too narrow in my description. Somewhere along the line, around 1961 or 1962, Leo Lerman called us on the phone and said, "We're printing a picture of The Living Theatre staff, and we're trying to caption it. Can you give me twenty words summing up the purpose of The Living Theatre?"

I said, "Call me back in five minutes." Quick consultation. He did call back in five minutes, not ten. I said, *"To increase conscious awareness, to stress the sacredness of life, to break down the walls."*

Fifteen words. *Doctor Faustus* had stressed the sacredness of life—that's what it was about. So did *Faustina, Ubu, Desire*. The description we gave Lerman that day has always been appropriate. Only now we know it. And so does our audience.

Jarry's *Ubu the King* was the last thing we did at the Cherry Lane. It was on a double bill with John Ashbery's *The Heroes*. Both plays debunked royalty. We produced them under even worse financial circumstances than *Desire*. *Desire* had opened at a cost of about thirty-five dollars. None of the actors were paid. I mean thirty-five dollars for the sets and costumes, but there were expenses for advertising, rent, printing, insurance, and the other things you forget about, especially if, like the rent, they have been paid in advance. *Ubu* cost even less. A massive show: I think there were about 150 costumes, seventeen sets. But we made the costumes out of old rags; the set was made of wrapping paper gleaned from the streets and pasted together. It was sumptuous. Nobody got paid, half the company slept in the theatre, and Sam Thau on Second Avenue fed the company free every night in his restaurant for weeks. He was later mysteriously killed.

The advantages of doing plays with little or no money far surpass the disadvantages. First of all, second of all, and last of all, you are outside of the money system. Because money is a brig. Better the slave of poverty than the minion of money. At least you're not being screwed all the time, distastefully, against your will, without love. The chief disadvantage is that, having to do everything yourself, it takes more time. The period of creativity preceding the opening of a production reaches its peak of intensity during the few weeks immediately preceding the opening itself. Creative juices, time. They just don't flow for long. The problem of working without money is that of sustaining the juice time. The fear is that you will be all drained before the end of the work. Then you have to implore the muse. May she be kindly disposed. I have found that she usually is, happily enough, whenever there is less of Mammon's largesse lying around.

The Cherry Lane was closed by the Fire Department. The loft on One Hundredth Street was closed by the Building Department. The theatre on Fourteenth Street was closed by the Internal Revenue Service. As a matter of fact, the very first theatre we had ever planned, The Wooster Stage, 1946, and this may be the first mention of it in print, was closed before it ever opened, by the Police Department. Somehow it is that way with us. At The Wooster Stage, located in a basement on Wooster Street, we had planned to do, among other things, some of the Pound-Fenellosa versions of the Noh. The theatre was to have been run on a membership basis only, a kind of club theatre. But the Police insisted that it was a front for a brothel. We were at that time too weak to fight back—we always lose anyway—

and we wrote Pound and told him about it, and he replied, "How else cd a seeryus tee-ater support itself in N.Y.?"

Wonder if that was in the back of my mind when I, years later, 1964, first used the minion image in the preceding paragraph.

We left the Cherry Lane trailing debts. We wanted to work free of the money madness and so decided on the loft, where we would not advertise, would not invite the critics, would not charge admission. The voluntary contributions averaged fifty-nine cents per spectator and that was enough to pay for everything, because there weren't any debts when the loft closed. But the sad part was that there never was enough money to pay the actors and all the rehearsing had to be done at night or on weekends and Judith and I were holding down daytime jobs, too. We never found it harassing but resented the inevitable break in concentration. When you put on a play you become obsessed with it. Everything else goes, eating, sleeping, attending to anything but the work at hand. Holding down a job splits the necessary concentration. That was why when the loft was closed we decided that we had to have a theatre which would at least pay the actors and us enough to get along on. It didn't always do that.

The experiments at the loft were mostly frail. That is, I cannot regard Strindberg's *The Spook Sonata* or Cocteau's *Orpheus* as experiments. We did them as experiments. That is, we scrupulously applied the rule that the director's function is to keep diving until the author's intentions are known and drawn to the light, realized, that nothing happens on the stage that does not support and develop as fully as possible the substance of the play. In a sense, to do the play honestly, no matter how taxing the demands of the script. The plays emerged, both of them casting spells that had us all in thrall. And here were two plays, both in prose, the highly personal prose of each author, involved, intensely personal, uncommon, called weird sometimes—in *Orpheus* some laughter, in *Spook* none—yet they worked. The clue here was the magic mystery, indeed the surreal quality, weaving in and out of lunches and suppers, glaziers who fly and mummies who talk, the uncanny, like Frankenstein, close to horror, and which chills the flesh. The clue: they made something disquieting happen to the spectator's body as he watched.

Pirandello's *Tonight We Improvise* was the first play since *Faustina* that we did which made a direct attempt at involving the audience. Of course, that is the heart of the Pirandello play. This device, the play within the play, the play that presumably takes place in the theatre on the night of the performance for the first time, as if it were the first time on each successive night, is part of a large part of twentieth-century dramatic literature. It cropped up again in *Many Loves*, and again in *The Connection*. And when, on Fourteenth Street, we revived *Improvise* and ran it in repertory with *Many Loves* and *The Connection*, all three of them with authors or directors running all over the theatre and large sections of the play taking place on the stage and in the audience, many people began to think that this was the message of The Living Theatre. We did not choose these plays because they contained these devices. It is true that our message, if you want to call it that, or our mission, was to involve or touch or engage the audience, not just show them something; but we did realize that these play-within-the-play devices arose out of a crying need on the part of the authors, and of us, to reach the audience, to awaken them from their passive slumber, to provoke them into attention, shock them if necessary, and, this is also important, to involve the actors with what was happening in the audience. To aid the audience to become once more what it was destined to be when the first dramas formed themselves on the threshing floor: a congregation led by priests, a choral ecstasy of reading and response, dance, seeking transcendence, a way out and up, the vertical thrust, seeking a state of awareness that surpasses mere conscious being and brings you closer to God. By bringing the play into the theatre and mixing together spectator and performer, the intention was to equalize, unify, and bring everyone closer to life. Joining as opposed to separation.

That there is no difference between actor and spectator. The Greeks used masks, and the Japanese, the Chinese, the *commedia,* and so many others, of course, but perhaps that is what we least need now. The mask has a function, but we had better learn that its purpose is not to conceal and symbolize, but to intensify, magnify, terrify, or seduce. I love masks but I love the human face more. I wonder about masks all the time. For instance, they almost work in Genet's *The Blacks* because the idea in that play is so repellent. Genet, I know, likes masks just as he likes velvet, fans, and gaudy colors, all the ostentation of extreme theatricalism all at once; his is an art of piling up extravagance on top of extravagance until the coagulated energy precipitates an explosion that brings freedom. In *The Screens,* too, he calls for masks, but I prefer the human face. Sometimes the secret of Genet's masks, and that may be why they work, is that the characters who wear them really do wear them in life, in the situation which they are enacting, and the sight of those masks makes us love all the more the human face which they hide. What is the function of a mask? This is still one of my unanswered questions.

People were often taken in by the play-within-the-play devices of *Many Loves, The Connection,* and *Improvise.* Not once, but often, people requested their money back at the box office because they had not come to see a bunch of people rehearsing; they wanted to see a show, the finished product. People theatrically unsophisticated, but to whom else are we speaking? Are we only addressing those in the know?

That part was good, that is, that people were disturbed and were learning. But the greater part of the spectators, the sophisticated spectators, were not content, particularly with the devices as employed by Gelber and Williams. Pirandello was more successful at it, probably because he concentrated on the humor of the situation and the confusion. Gelber and Williams were more sententious. But we were finally disturbed ourselves by the device because it was, after all, basically dishonest, and we were publicly crying out for honesty in the theatre. The plays were not being rehearsed that night yet we were pretending they were.

Night after night, night after night, several hundred times in fact, the audience applauded whenever the actor playing the producer in *The Connection* said, "And this is Jaybird, the author of *The Connection*." They weren't applauding because they were playing the game but because they were taken in. Fraud. Same thing with *Many Loves*. Deception was not the means we wanted to involve the audience. It fundamentally meant that we did not respect the people out there. You do not cheat when you respect, and when the audience found out, and it surely would find out, it would not respect us for having fooled them, no matter how well we had done it.

The climax of our work at the loft was Paul Goodman's *The Young Disciple*, half in verse and half in prose. But Goodman knew what he was about, he always does, and in this play, among other things, he was confronting the problem of verse in the theatre, and in his brief preface to it he writes:

I have tried in this play to lay great emphasis on the pre-verbal elements of theatre, trembling, beating, breathing hard, and tantrum. I am well aware that the actors we have are quite unable both by character and training to open their throats to such sounds or loosen their limbs to such motions. But this is also why they simply cannot read poetic lines. It would be worth-while, to the renovation of our art, to make a number of plays of just these pre-verbal elements in abstraction, as the painters have returned to the elements of color and form.

Is the solution as plain as Goodman says? If so, then let us get to work at once. I know that if it is not all of the solution it is part, one of the wheels of the way. What happened when we did this play was exciting for us. Apparently also for the audience. They were disgusted, affronted, annoyed, terrified, awed, and excited. There is a scene in which a character vomits, and one in which someone creeps about on all fours in total darkness making night noises, strange husky grating and chirping sounds, and the audience panicked, and something was happening which whispered to us that it was important.

Before the new theatre opened on Fourteenth Street, while we were remodeling the building, Grove Press brought out M. C. Richards' translation of Artaud's *The Theatre and Its Double*. Paul reviewed it for *The Nation*. I don't know if he was familiar with Artaud's theories prior to that time, but I do know that, whether or not he was, what he had accomplished in *The Young Disciple* was fraught with intimations of a Theatre of Cruelty.

M. C. sent us a copy of the book before publication, in the summer of 1958, and we opened it and read one line and quickly read it from start to finish, and then again and again. The ghost of Artaud became our mentor and the problem that we faced as we began our work on Fourteenth Street was how to create that spectacle, that Aztec, convulsive, plague-ridden panorama that would so shake people up, so move them, so cause feeling to be felt, there in the body, that the steel world of law and order which civilization had forged to protect itself from barbarism would melt. Why? Because that steel world of law and order did more than just protect us from barbarism; it also cut us off from real feeling. That is, in the process of protecting ourselves from the barbaric instincts and acts we feared, we simultaneously cut ourselves off from all impulsive sensation and made ourselves the heartless monsters that wage wars, that burn and gas six million Jews, that enslave the blacks, that plan bacteriological weapons, that annihilate Carthage and Hiroshima, that humiliate and crush, that conduct inquisitions, that hang men in cages to die of starvation and exposure there in that great concourse of the Piazza San Marco, that wipe out the Indians, the buffalo, that exploit the peon, that lock men in prisons away from natural sex, that invent the gallows, the garrote, the block, the guillotine, the electric chair, the gas chamber, the firing squad, that take young men in their prime and deliberately teach them to kill—I mean we actually teach people to kill—and that go about our daily business while one person every six seconds dies of starvation. Artaud believed that if we could only be made to feel, really feel anything, then we might find all this suffering intolerable, the pain too great to bear, we might put an end to it, and then, being able to feel, we might truly feel the joy, the joy of everything else, of loving, of creating, of being at peace, and of being ourselves.

Jack Gelber brought us *The Connection* in the spring of 1958 when we were preparing the Fourteenth Street theatre. I opened it, looked at a line, and sat down and read it instantly. Gave it to Judith who immediately wanted to direct it, and we decided that day that we would do it.

First, we did *Many Loves*. It had been the last public event at the loft. We had done a reading of it there, and since the time that we had had the Cherry Lane, we had been waiting for the proper moment to put it on a stage. It seemed appropriate for the opening of the new theatre. Also a good risk. Curious for me to admit this, but it was the fact. And like so many of the plays we have worked on, it was a palimpsest, with many layers of meaning, like the world, no one story, but many, involved and interconnected, and most of all disconnected, but all happening at the same time, speaking of things high and unreachable and things buried, equally unreachable. And the whole question of verse in the theatre was put before the audience. It was much of the subject matter of the interplay between the author, producer, and actress, and tied the play together structurally. The contrast of verse and prose began to show how speech that was extraordinary and elevated could also be clear and simple and acceptable for daily life. A new indication.

In July of that year we opened *The Connection*. Our planning had been smart. The play received its renowned

bad notices, and by running it in repertory with *Many Loves*
we carried it through to the fall when the good notices arrived. *The Connection* kept the rest of the repertory going
for the next two years.

Insert. Repertory. I have nothing to say about repertory
that has not been said before. There can be no creative, that
is, growing, company of actors without it; the one-shot stuff
is merely obeisance to Mammon's dynasty, and so forth.

We, who had sought to develop style through variations of
formal staging, found suddenly in the free movement and
the true improvisation of *The Connection* something we
had not formerly considered.

A resurgence of realism was needed: what had been
passing for realism was not real. There had to be pauses.
Directors had to learn to let actors sit still for a long time
in one place as in life, and actors had to learn to adapt to
this new idea. There had to be an end to sets with angled
walls, the whole false perspective bit. There had to be real
dirt, not simulations. There had to be slovenly speech. If
there was to be jazz, then it had to be real jazz and not
show-tune jazz. If there was to be real speech, then there
had to be real profanity; the word "shit" would have to be
said, not once but again and again and again until audience
ears got used to it. Goodman has been using words like
"shit," "cock," "cunt," and "fuck" in his theatre pieces for
more than a decade. The way had been prepared, and he
had used the words not as expletives but as functional Anglo-
Saxon words in context. Of course, that was intolerable. But
Gelber's unrelenting and uncompromising use of the word
"shit" in its most ordinary usage would make it easier for
the Goodman plays in the future. There had to be honesty,
as much honesty as we could pull out. We had to risk em-
barrassment; we had to risk boring the audience, but it had
to be done. We had to talk about the untalkable subjects;
we had to talk about heroin and addicts. It was important,
important to show that these people who, in 1959, were
considered the lowest of the low—in fact a recent law had

made selling heroin to minors a capital offense—we had to show that these, the dregs of society as they were regarded, were human, capable of deep and touching feelings and speech, worthy of our interest and respect; we had to show that we were all in need of a fix, and that what the addicts had come to was not the result of an indigenous personality evil, but was symptomatic of the errors of the whole word.

Almost fifty men fainted during the run of *The Connection*, not only in America but when we played it in Europe, too. Always around the same point. The overdose. Not one admitted it. They always said, as they regained consciousness on the lobby floor, "It was hot and stuffy in there," "I felt ill all day," "I was overtired," "I ate something that didn't agree with me," "It's nothing," "No, it wasn't the play," never the play. But we did have smelling salts on hand. And if it was the sight of the needle that made them faint, then maybe by jabbing away we'll get somewhere.

The work of John Cage. We first became acquainted with it around 1950. The first concern, the first special event ever presented by The Living Theatre, was arranged by him at the Cherry Lane. We presented the première of his *Music of Changes*. By using methods of chance and indeterminacy to construct his work, he was saying to us all, "Get rid of all this misdirected conscious dominion. Let the wind blow through. See what can happen without the government of sweet reason." These methods produced remarkable effects in his music. We had all been long familiar with the effects of chance in painting: Arp's "Pieces of Paper Arranged According to the Laws of Chance," Duchamps' great glass which splintered so beautifully by accident, Kandinsky's and Picasso's and Pollack's accidental drips and splashes. In *The Connection* Judith had arranged an atmosphere in which the actors could improvise lines and actions, in the context of the play, never straying too far. This often led to terrible choices, largely because we are not well trained in this area, but often terrific moments emerged. Best of all, an atmosphere of freedom in the performance was established and encouraged, and this seemed to promote a truthfulness, startling in performance, which we had not so thoroughly produced before. With the readdition to the repertory of *Tonight We Improvise*, improvisation, of which chance is a major constituent, began to be identified with the work of The Living Theatre. We permitted the description and encouraged it, hoping we could find a play in which we could improvise boldly, in which we could let the wind blow through, and let things happen that had not been predesigned.

Jackson MacLow's *The Marrying Maiden*. This whole play had been constructed by MacLow with methods he had himself invented out of inspiration derived from the work of Cage. The process used to make *The Marrying Maiden* was described by Judith in her program notes for the play.

The author used as the vocabulary of *The Marrying Maiden* words or groups of words from *The Book of Changes* (in Cary F. Baynes's translation of Richard Wilhelm's rendition of the *I Ching*, published by the Bollingen Foundation). In addition to the vocabulary, the author supplied the division into speeches, scenes and characters, and a series of directions consisting of five gradations of loud and soft, five gradations of fast and slow, and several hundred adverbs and adverbial phrases suggestive of actors' readings. All these were derived by the author by chance operational systems and were interspersed at very close intervals within the vocabulary to give the play of changes its volatile quality.

The director supplied the scenario, which was not determined by chance procedures but by her personal choice of ideography. The director also conceived of the method of using the "action pack." The "action pack" itself was supplied by the author and the actions indicated on the cards were by the author. The cards and their use were determined by the throw of the dice.

The role of the Dice Thrower is specially conceived by the director for Henry Proach. The director thought of the character of the Dice Thrower as Fate, or, in its largest sense, as the Stage Manager.

The score and the idea for the score were by John Cage, to whom we owed more than the sound track, for his work on chance and indeterminacy has been fundamental in the inspiration of both author and director. The use of the score was determined by the throw of the dice.

Well, what was going on on the stage was pretty wild. Every time the Dice Thrower rolled a seven he pulled out a card from the action pack and brought it to the actor who was to speak next. The actor then had to incorporate the action written on the card into whatever he was about to do as determined by the scenario. Every time the Dice Thrower rolled a five he turned on the music, which was a hi-fi recording of the actors reading the play. Sometimes you could hear a tape of the actor speaking and at the same time the actor actually speaking. Every time the Dice Thrower rolled another five he turned the sound off. Now we were really improvising, no faking at all. Things were beginning to happen on our stage which had never happened before. Each performance was different from the next, and the production was a notorious failure. We insisted on keeping the play in repertory for almost a year, usually playing it only once a week, usually to no more than ten or twenty persons. Not arrogance, but a stubborn belief that we needed the play, we the company, that it had something to teach us if only we could stick with it.

But it frightened us, too. The next play we did was Brecht's *In the Jungle of Cities*. The whole production was scientifically charted. Every moment, every sound cue, and there were more than 150 of them in Teiji Ito's score, every position of every prop and bit of intricate scenery was plotted and continually placed with scrupulous precision. It was Brecht's second play, written by him at the same age at which Gelber wrote *The Connection*. The political overtones of the play were not apparent to many, but we grooved with what Brecht was saying. It is a play about money and the corruption it produces. It turns the innocent romantic young man, Garga, into a demon, and the loss of money restores to the gang-leading Shlink the wisdom of the Orient which Brecht so thoroughly respected.

The levels of meaning were plentiful and the language and action of the play were deeply influenced by Rimbaud and the then rising school of surrealism. Brecht quotes whole stretches from *A Season in Hell*. The play had the color and magic mystery that we had found in Strindberg and Cocteau, and like most of Brecht's work it was epic in concept and structure. It was well received and the company loved playing it. It was a relief from the uncertainty of *The Maiden*, and a relief from the scorn which had greeted it. Besides we were doing Brecht, the first successful production of any of his plays in New York. I'm not talking about *The Three Penny Opera*, because Weill's contribution makes it something else than straight drama. We all knew that Brecht always meant a political statement, and actors love Brecht because Brecht loves his characters. True villains are few in Brecht. It is the system, not the men.

Also, the free style of staging, which Judith had begun in *The Connection*, was used with equal skill in staging *The Jungle*. She began to let the actors design their movements, creating a remarkable rehearsal atmosphere in which the company became more and more free to bring in its own ideas. Less and less puppetry, more and more the creative actor. The careful directing books we had used at the beginning were by now quite gone. She began to suggest rather than tell, and the company began to find a style that was not superimposed but rose out of their own sensitivities. The director was resigning from his authoritarian position. No more dictation.

Still searching for Artaud. We also talked publicly a good deal about the theatre being like a dream in which the spectator is the dreamer and from which he emerges remembering it with partial understanding. We had talked about this with Paul Williams, who designed the Fourteenth Street theatre for us. That is why the lobby was painted so brightly, the brick walls exposed, like the walls of a courtyard, the ceiling painted sky blue, a fountain running as in a public square, and kiosks standing in the center, one for coffee and one for books. The lobby was the day room, the theatre was painted black, narrower and narrower stripes converging toward the stage, concentrating the focus, as if one were inside an old-fashioned Kodak, looking out through the lens, the eye of the dreamer in the dark room. The seats were painted in hazy gray, lavender, and sand, with oversize circus numbers on them in bright orange, lemon and magenta—all this Williams' attempt to aid us to achieve an atmosphere for the dreamers and their waking-up when they walked out into the lobby.

Gelber's *The Apple* was a nightmare play, laden with symbols, the kind that baffle you in dreams. He tried harder than ever before to involve the audience in the action, and, still further, he wanted to produce horror and cold terror. Ferocious scenes: a mad dentist spiking the patient and drilling away to "The Flight of the Bumble Bee"; people turning into insects: suddenly huge black ants or flapping butterflies; a tormented spastic dancing with another man; insults, jibes, loathsome anti-Semitic, anti-Negro, anti-Oriental, white Protestant American remarks. A whole dictionary of revulsion, all in this form that kept switching from dream to coffee-shop reality, from the stage into the theatre itself. But the horror remained on the stage, somehow, swathed somehow in the dream. The language was inventive, incomprehensible to many, but measured, every word carefully considered—I know how Jack and Judith worried over each syllable—nothing left to chance there. The horror was mixed with fantasy. Important to remember.

We returned to Brecht. *Man Is Man.* Here Brecht's political commitment is no longer vague. It's all about identity and its usurpation by the power structure for its own ends, the dehumanizing effects of authority, the state, the army, and the old lady of Threadneedle Street, the Bank of England, the Economy, Widow Begbick.

Popularly interpreted in the press as a play about brainwashing, the majority deliberately missed the point and pretended.it applied solely to Communist techniques in Korea or some foreign part.

How to break through. We wanted to do the play fiercely. After all, Brecht, like Shaw, made some kind of fatal error. Both had something to say about the socioeconomic political state of things. Both believed that you couldn't really talk altogether straight to the audience about these things, that the spectators would be bored and walk out. Both had their own methods for coating the pill. Shaw with his wit, Brecht with his divertisements: all the effects, turntables, slides, multiple scenes, choruses, exotic geography, songs, painted faces, snowfalls, rainstorms, parades, his endless engaging distractions and excitements. These things are always loved, always admired, as are Shaw's wit and technique. The pill, the medicine, the audience always spits out. We tried to do *Man Is Man* in such a way that there would be no coating, to cope with the alienation. What is that all about? It is to cut off sentiment, crying about the wrong things, things not befitting the miracle of tears. It is really to get people to look at things clearly, examine them minutely, just as Brecht's characters do, and then to do what Brecht's characters do, which is to slip back into the action. Galy Gay and Widow Begbick come forward to the front of the stage. They know what it is all about, they see it clearly. And then like the humans we all are, they let themselves be sucked back into the action to commit the mistakes they know will be mistakes.

The subject matter of *Man Is Man* is the same subject matter as *The Brig*, which arrived in the mail while *Man Is Man* was running. I opened the play, read a line, read the whole thing that night—Judith, too—and it was clear that it would be the next play we would do.

Everything always seems to connect, everything in my life

leading to the moment when *The Brig* arrived and enabled me to gasp and know that here it was, that if I were to avoid it, I would be rejecting my course, losing the splendor, if it is that, when it all coheres. Pound.

Brown, in a brig in Japan, staring straight ahead at attention or exhausted falling asleep at night, but with a writer's canny feel, said to himself, "What a thing all this is." And getting out of the place, he made accurate diagrams of the architecture and tried first to cast the happenings into the form of a novel, but his instincts sharpened and he turned it into "A concept for the stage or film."

In it, not by Brown's design, but by some other design, are all the things which constitute the history of The Living Theatre's direction. And of me, and Judith, and perhaps all of us. The search for exactness, pinnacle. The search for strict formalism in the very nature of the action, the elements of choreography and of music, of rhythm. In all the improvisations, the indeterminate scenes that could result from a missing button on a costume, an accidental slip of a foot, the search for a Theatre of Chance. In its focus on the crime of self-abasement, a major clue to what we have to do. In its vehement exposure of the human attrition wrought by authority was a complete critique of the damaging force of our society. In the reverence for truly spoken speech, the reverence clear by the absence of just such speech and the few phrases of friendly conversation, thick hints of the new poetry we are seeking.

The Brig condemned and exposed the barricades which divide us into victims or executioners. Barricades, a play of barricades, a play of prisons, prisons which have entered briefly yet decisively into our experience, Judith's and mine. Prisons haunt. I think once in, you never get out, never get prison out of your bones, not until the last one falls.

When I read *The Brig* I imagined the noise of the shouting, the marching, the stamping of feet in that brig prison, and I projected it onto The Living Theatre's stage. There was a mysterious compulsion to bring that prison noise into the room where once the memory of it had killed the applause. Let the audience hear it, too.

To break down the walls. How can you watch *The Brig* and not want to break down the walls of all the prisons? Free all prisoners. Destroy all white lines everywhere. All the barriers. But talking about this to people is not enough. To make people feel so that whenever the noise of triumph is heard, the noise of opening night applause, no other noise can be heard but the terrible noise in the resounding cement and steel corridors of prisons, let them hear the noise, let it cause them pain, let them feel the blows to the stomach, produce a horror and release real feeling, let this happen until there are no prisons anywhere.

The Brig is the Theatre of Cruelty. In that it is the distillation of the direction of The Living Theatre's history. You cannot shut off from it, as from a dream. It is there, real, in the pit of your stomach. Defy the audience. Tell them you don't want to involve them. Don't run into the aisle to embrace them. Put up a barricade of barbed wire. Separate until the pain of separation is felt, until they want to tear it down, to be united. Storm the barricades.

When we were arrested for insisting on putting on our play, Judith, myself, Ken Brown, so many members of the cast and staff, and when we were brought to trial, one of the charges in the indictment was that we had yelled, "Storm the barricades!" from a window to the crowd in the street below waiting to be let in to see the last performance of *The Brig*. We were acquitted of that charge. Rightly so; we never said it. Never said it because we are simply too familiar with public demonstrations and the responsibility of leaders of demonstrations, too committed to the Gandhiian concept of nonviolence ever to incite a crowd in this manner, but when the suggestion of this charge first confronted me at a grand jury hearing, I went through a twisting moment of *déjà vu* or *déjà entendu*. Where did this accusation come from? The Assistant U.S. Attorney was asking me, "Mr.

Beck, did you or did you not shout 'Storm the barricades!'?"

"No," I stumbled a reply, "no."

At the trial no one could testify that either of us, Judith or I, had said this, though someone who was on our side said that the words might have passed his lips; so maybe that's the explanation. But all that night I felt we were confronting the barricades. Yes, we want to get rid of all the barricades, even our own and any that we might ever set up.

The Brig and Artaud. Artaud's mistake was that he imagined you could create a horror out of the fantastic. Brown's gleaming discovery is that horror is not in what we imagine but is in what is real.

JULIAN BECK

New York City
July 1964

PRODUCTIONS OF
THE LIVING THEATRE

CHERRY LANE

Four Plays: August 15, 1951
  Childish Jokes by Paul Goodman
  Ladies' Voices by Gertrude Stein
  He Who Says Yes and He Who Says
    No by Bertolt Brecht
  The Dialogue of the Manikin and
    the Young Man by F. Garcia Lorca
Doctor Faustus Lights the Lights   December 2, 1951
  by Gertrude Stein
Beyond the Mountains   December 30, 1951
  by Kenneth Rexroth
An Evening of Bohemian Theatre: March 2, 1952
  Desire Trapped by the Tail by Pablo
    Picasso
  Ladies' Voices by Gertrude Stein
  Sweeney Agonistes by T. S. Eliot
Faustina by Paul Goodman   May 25, 1952
Ubu the King by Alfred Jarry and   August 5, 1952
  The Heroes by John Ashbery

ONE HUNDREDTH STREET

The Age of Anxiety by W. H. Auden	March 18, 1954
The Spook Sonata by August Strindberg	June 3, 1954
Orpheus by Jean Cocteau	September 30, 1954
The Idiot King by Claude Fredericks	December 2, 1954
Tonight We Improvise by Luigi Pirandello	February 17, 1955
Phèdre by Jean Racine	May 27, 1955
The Young Disciple by Paul Goodman	October 12, 1955
Many Loves by William Carlos Williams	January 13, 1959
The Cave at Machpelah	June 30, 1959
by Paul Goodman	

FOURTEENTH STREET

The Connection by Jack Gelber	July 15, 1959
Tonight We Improvise by Luigi Pirandello	November 6, 1959

The Theatre of Chance: June 22, 1960
    The Marrying Maiden
        by Jackson MacLow
    Women of Trachis by Sophokles/Pound
In the Jungle of Cities by Bertolt Brecht   December 20, 1960
The Apple by Jack Gelber   December 7, 1961
Man Is Man by Bertolt Brecht   September 18, 1962
The Brig by Kenneth H. Brown   May 15, 1963

THE BRIG

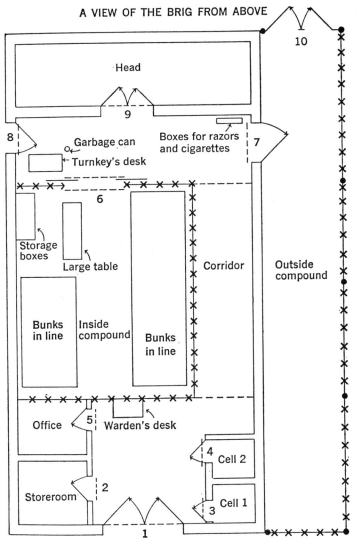

A VIEW OF THE BRIG FROM ABOVE

Head

10

8

Garbage can

← Turnkey's desk

Boxes for razors and cigarettes

7

9

6

Storage boxes

Large table

Corridor

Outside compound

Bunks in line

Inside compound

Bunks in line

Office

5

Warden's desk

4 Cell 2

Storeroom

2

3 Cell 1

1

1. Large double doors
2. Storeroom door
3. Door to cell no. 1
4. Door to cell no. 2
5. Door to office
6. Door to inside compound
7. Door to outside compound
8. Freedom door
9. Head door
10. Large double gates

—————— Concrete wall
—x—x—x— Heavy Chicken wire
- - - - - - - White line

NOTES

Time: March 1957
Place: Japan

At the foot of Mount Fujiyama in central Japan, there was an American Marine infantry unit known as the Third Marines. Sometime in March 1957, the entire unit left the vicinity for Okinawa. In the center of an area of two square miles, enclosed with barbed wire, containing many single-level, green, wooden, cement-floored barracks and a lesser number of conventional Quonset huts, there was a singular green wooden building that was smaller than the rest. This was the penal institution of the organization, known as the Brig. Because of its reputation as a place of horrible extremes of discipline and order, it was feared and ignored by members of the unit not directly connected with it. It stood as an example of consequence to those who would not, could not, or wished not to conform to the rigid routine of the Third Marines.

Orientation: The building was rectangular in all the proportions of its construction. It was, like most other buildings in the camp, wooden framed, painted green, and cement floored. The walls, from ground level to ceiling, were fifteen feet high and the convex sheet-metal roof raised the over-all height of the building to twenty-five feet. The side, or longest, walls were forty yards long, while the front and rear walls were twenty yards wide. The front wall contained a six-foot window in each side and large double doors in the center. Each side wall was identical, containing six windows of dimensions similar to those in the front and one windowless door about ten yards from the rear of the building. The rear wall was blank. Every window was barred.

Looking from front to rear, on the right side of the building was a yard enclosed in a barbed-wire fence some twenty feet high. The fence was connected to that side of the building. The yard ran the length of the Brig and was twenty

43

yards in width. It was accessible by the door in the rear of
that side of the building and by enormous double gates at
the rear of the fence, which were secured by a tremendous
lock connected to a chain.

The inside of the building from front to rear was constructed thus: Entering through the large double doors, there
was a corridor about fifteen feet wide. The corridor was twenty
feet long and on the right of it were two square concrete
cells called simply one and two. These were for especially
incorrigible prisoners. They had conventional steel-barred
doors and measured ten by eight by six feet. On the left side
of the corridor was a room ten by fifteen by twenty feet, containing soap, buckets, scrub brushes, brooms, dustpans, paint,
rags, and all manner of paraphernalia necessary to the opera-
tion of a brig. This was called the storeroom. Farther down
the left side of the corridor was the Brig officers' office;
where the standard operative procedure was developed. In
the center of the end of the corridor was a desk where a
senior sergeant known as The Warden sat. He concerned
himself with the everyday running of the place, dealing with
admissions, releases, punishments, and miscellaneous problems as they arose. He was the disciplinarian and actual boss
of procedure, carrying out the intructions of his superiors.
Beyond the desk of The Warden was an area twenty yards
long and eighteen yards wide, enclosed from floor to ceiling
in chicken wire. The wire ran from the left wall to within
eight feet of the right wall, permitting a corridor to the right
of it. Inside the wire were fifteen double army cots, nine on
the right and six on the left. In the space remaining on the
left side was a long wooden mess-type table with connected
planks for sitting. On the wall to the left of the table were
forty wooden, frontless boxes built into the wall. Those in
use were numbered, each containing five pair of socks, five
sets of underwear, an extra set of shoes and dungarees, two
towels, and the toilet articles of the prisoners.

On the far side of the enclosure was an area about ten
yards square containing a desk parallel to the mess-type table

and just to the other side of the chicken wire. This was the turnkey's desk. He was a corporal, and was responsible for all activity in this area of the building. On left side of the rear wall of this area of the Brig was a blackboard on which were written the names, assigned numbers (each prisoner was called by number rather than name), expiration dates of prison terms, and a point demerit system to make evident the most and least co-operative inmates. In the center of this wall was the door to the lavatory. On the right side was a cabinet containing forty miniature boxes of the same design as those on the wall within the sleeping area. Each box in use was similarly numbered and contained the cigarettes, razors, and razor blades of each prisoner.

There were four doors in this area—
1. The outside door, which led to the yard. (Right.)
2. The freedom door, which led to the outside world. (Left.)
3. The door to the head or lavatory. (Rear center.)
4. The steel-framed chicken-wire door, which led to the sleeping area. (Front center.)

The following titles were given to the following areas—
1. The outside compound: The fenced in outside area.
2. The compound: The caged area inside the Brig.
3. Post One: The narrow corridor beside the compound and the forward section of the Brig.
4. Post Two: The area to the rear of the compound and the head.

Brig Regulations—
1. No prisoner may speak at any time except to his guards. A prisoner must request permission to do any and everything in the following way: "Sir, prisoner Number — requests permission to speak, sir." He must speak in a loud, clear, impersonal, and unaffected tone.
2. At each exit and entrance there is a white line. No prisoner may cross any white line without requesting permission to do so in the manner quoted above.

3. When unassigned a prisoner shall, at all times, stand at attention in front of his bunk and read *The Guidebook for Marines,* which will be found at the head of his bunk between his field jacket and cap. The towel and laundry bag of each prisoner hangs at the rear of his bunk.

4. No prisoner shall sit down at any time unless it is necessary for the completion of an assigned task.

5. Under no circumstances shall a prisoner be permitted to walk from place to place. He must run, or, if this is not practical, he must at least show evidence of a trot.

6. The hair of the prisoners shall be cut identically in a short crew cut.

7. The uniform of each prisoner shall be identical. The prisoner wears a white T-shirt and trunk-type underpants. He wears clean but wrinkled dungarees, which he washes twice a week at a community wash. All buttons must be sewed properly in place and buttoned at all times. He wears a web belt with a brass buckle. His dungaree cap is worn only outside the building. When entering or leaving the Brig, he must raise his right leg and snap the cap on his thigh to insure that it contains no object. He wears green woolen socks and combat boots that must show no evidence of polish. His coat for cold and inclement weather is a standard field jacket.

8. Each time a prisoner returns from outside, he shall be searched by a guard or a delegation of guards. The extent of the search is up to the discretion of the senior guard.

> a. If the guard should say, "Break down for a frisk," the prisoner shall open all buttons of his clothing and his shoelaces and stand at attention facing the chicken wire, with his hat in his right hand. (All searching is done in the corridor next to the compound.) When a guard stands behind a prisoner in this position, the prisoner shall snap his hat on his right thigh, throw his arms out and above his head, and fall forward about three feet, gripping the wire high and hard. His legs must

be far apart. The prisoner is searched in this position, and when the guard is finished, he slaps the prisoner on the leg. The prisoner then resumes his original position, fastens his clothing, and waits to be dismissed.

b. If the guard should say, "Break down for a shake-down," the prisoner shall remove all clothing except his socks and underwear, placing clothing in a pile in front of him, and standing at attention until a guard stands in front of the pile. Then the prisoner shall hold the articles, one by one, in the following order, with both hands, directly in front of his person: the field jacket, held by the shoulders; the dungaree jacket, held by the shoulders; the trousers, held at the waist; the cap, in the right hand; and the shoes, held at the heel. When the guard has searched all the articles, he will walk away from the prisoner and the prisoner shall dress.

9. The uniform of the guards is tight-fitting, standard Marine Corps khaki with the overseas cap. They wear no tie, and the throat of the uniform is open, showing a line of white T-shirt. They wear a wide, white combat belt with an eight-inch billy club attached and black, highly polished shoes.

10. The voices of the guards, when speaking to the prisoners, shall be of a deep and authoritative tone. Cynicism, sarcasm, and conviction shall vary to extreme degrees according to what is said.

CHARACTERS

The Guards

TEPPERMAN, *a tall, heavily built Negro with a New York accent. Twenty-one years old. He wears one stripe on his uniform*

GRACE, *a short and stocky Midwesterner. Twenty-two years old. He wears two stripes on his uniform*

THE WARDEN, *a well-built man of medium height with a slight Southern accent. Thirty years old. He wears four stripes on his uniform*

LINTZ, *a blond, tall, and slightly built Californian. Nineteen years old. He wears one stripe on his uniform*

The Prisoners

In all, there are eleven prisoners, which make up a cross-section of American society.

ONE, *a thin and sickly boy of eighteen*

TWO, *a tall, dark, and handsome young man of twenty-one*

THREE, *a seedy, short, and rather stupid-looking Negro of twenty-five*

FOUR, *a tall and awkward boy of eighteen*

FIVE (the first), *a freckle-faced Irish lad of nineteen*

FIVE (the second), *a meticulous and powerful young man of twenty-one. Tall and intelligent*

SIX, *a rough-looking man of thirty-four*

SEVEN, *an inconspicuous and well-adjusted prisoner*

EIGHT, *a healthy country lad—Southern accent*

NINE, *an inconspicuous and well-adjusted prisoner*

TEN, *a squat, Southern tough of twenty-two*

Incidental Players

Two stretcher bearers

ACT ONE

SCENE 1

The inside of the Brig, four o'clock in the morning. In view are Post One, Post Two, and the inside compound.

The curtain opens to complete darkness. A dim colored light focuses on PFC. TEPPERMAN *standing at the desk of the turnkey,* CORPORAL GRACE, *who is seated there. They are whispering and smiling.* TEPPERMAN *walks to the door of the inside compound, unlocks it, and enters. He walks to the center of the sleeping area, takes his billy from his belt, and taps a prisoner, who is sleeping, on the head. Only this is visible, since the dim light has followed* TEPPERMAN.

TEPPERMAN. Wake up, Two. [*In a low, almost whispering, but stern tone.*] You better move, boy.

Two [*loud and clear*]. Yes, sir.

Tepperman. You better speak low, boy, when the lights are out in the compound. You want to wake up the other maggots? [*Pause.*] You better answer me, boy.

Two. Yes, sir. I mean no, sir.

Tepperman. I don't think you know what you mean, Two. Put your shoes on. Don't you know that bare feet never touch the deck? They make it greasy. [*Pause.*] Put your shoes on and report to me at the turnkey's desk. And don't request permission to cross the line, boy.

TEPPERMAN *leaves and the light follows him. He returns to the turnkey's desk. A moment later* Two *appears at attention at the desk, in his boots and underwear.*

49

Two. Sir, Prisoner Number Two reporting as ordered, sir.

Grace [*standing up quickly*]. What are your orders, Two?

Two. To report to your desk, sir.

Grace. You are a new maggot in my house, and I want to look at you. [*He walks around the prisoner.*] You are a mess, maggot, do you know that?

Two. Yes, sir.

Tepperman [*leaning toward the prisoner*]. Yes, yes, you, you are a mess, boy. Say it. Say you are a mess.

Two. Sir, I am a mess, sir.

Tepperman [*hitting the prisoner in the stomach repeatedly with his billy*]. I am going to be watching you among the rest of my lice, and if you are not squared away . . . [*Pauses, then smiling.*] I will clean up the deck with you. Is that clear, Two?

Two [*doubling over from the blows*]. Yes, sir.

Grace. Your guts are soft, maggot. Stand at attention. Nobody asked you to bend over. Stand up. You're making me sick with your little-girl tricks. That's better. [*Turning to* TEPPERMAN.] We've had enough of this new one. Send him back to his rack.

Tepperman. Split, maggot.

Two *does a military about-face and disappears in the darkness.*

Grace [*looking at his watch*]. It's almost time to get them up, Tep. Are you ready?

Tepperman [*smiling*]. Let me get my bugle.

TEPPERMAN *takes the cover from a tin garbage can next to the desk and walks to the door of the compound.* GRACE *flicks a switch on the wall near his desk, and suddenly the stage is bathed in light—bright, white, electric. At the moment the light goes on,* TEPPERMAN *crashes the can cover down the middle of the inside compound, making a resounding noise. In an instant, the prisoners are standing in front of their bunks at attention, in their underwear and boots, with all their bedclothes, sheets, pillow, and blanket rolled up in a ball in their arms.* GRACE *and* TEPPERMAN *walk up and down the aisle of the compound, studying the faces of the prisoners.* THE WARDEN *stands up, turns, and faces the compound and observes the proceedings with* LINTZ, *Post One, from the other side of the wire.*

The Warden. Good morning, kiddies. This will be another glorious day in the history of the United States Marine Corps. I want you to get dressed, make up your racks, get your soap and towels, and line up on the white line for washing your little handsies and facies. Is that clear?

All prisoners. Yes, sir.

The Warden. I can't hear you.

All prisoners. Yes, sir.

Warden. I still can't hear you.

All prisoners. Yes, sir.

Warden. Get hot.

At once there is a flourish of activity in the compound. The prisoners proceed to get dressed and get in each other's way as one makes the bottom bunk and one makes the top one. They make up their bunks in military fashion and take their field jackets, manuals, and caps from the floor, where they are put overnight, and place them at the head of their bunks. They then take their towels from the rear of their bunks, run to their respective numbered boxes, pick up a small plastic box containing soap, and form a line very close to one another standing at attention, the first man with his shoetips touching the white line inside the door to the compound.
The Brig falls silent once more.

Tepperman. Sound off.

The prisoners from front to rear in line begin to exclaim one at a time: "Sir, Prisoner Number One, sir," "Sir, Prisoner Number Two, sir." *And so on, through* NUMBER TEN.

Tepperman. All you maggots cross the white lines into the head, wash, and get in front of your racks on the double.

All the prisoners run into the head in single file. Moments later, they begin at the inside exit from the head to exclaim, one by one: "Sir, Prisoner Number One requests permission to cross the white line, sir," *and so on.* TEPPERMAN *stands at the door to the head and says,* "Cross," *as each one finishes this statement, using his own number. The prisoners then stop at the entrance to the compound and repeat the formality.* CORPORAL GRACE *is there uttering the same word,* "CROSS," *and the prisoners enter the compound, return their soap and towels and pick up their manuals, stand at attention in front of their racks, and begin to read. As the procession ends, with each prisoner at attention, reading,* TEPPERMAN *enters, goes to the blackboard on the rear wall, and studies it.*

Tepperman. Three get to the storeroom. One and Two head detail. Four sweep Post One. Five swab Post One. Six sweep Post Two. Seven swab Post Two. Eight sweep the compound. Nine swab the compound. Ten square away the boxes.

As TEPPERMAN *issues the orders, the Brig becomes a veritable madhouse: prisoners requesting to cross white lines, sweeping, swabbing, taking and returning materials from* THREE, *the storehouse man, and running in all directions. Two men disappear into the head with scouring powder, brushes, and rags. There is a line at the storeroom door with* THREE *standing inside giving and receiving buckets, brooms, swabs, and rags. Prisoners* FIVE, SEVEN, *and* NINE *run in and out of the head procuring buckets of water and emptying them, and the word* "CROSS" *is uttered many times by* THE WARDEN *and his three assistants as they walk about supervising the clean-up job. As the jobs begin to look accomplished,* THE WARDEN *conducts an inspection of the entire Brig. Soon all prisoners are reading in front of their bunks.*

The Warden. Secure all manuals and prepare for morning chow.

Lintz. Three, secure the storeroom and get in front of your rack ready for chow.

The prisoners put on their field jackets and take their caps in their right hands, and once again form a single line at the white line by the door of the compound. TEPPERMAN *opens the outside door and goes out into the outside compound.*

Grace. Outside in three ranks, move.

The prisoners run in single file through the outside door, snapping their hats on an uplifted right leg as they pass into the outside compound. The guards and THE WARDEN, *armed with shotguns which they took from the Brig officers' office, step through the outside door and close it. The Brig is empty and silent.*

Curtain.

SCENE 2

The outside compound. The curtain opens with the prisoners formed in two equal ranks at attention facing the long side of the fence with their backs to the wall of the Brig. Outside the fence stands LINTZ *with a shotgun cradled in his arms. It is about six o'clock in the morning and still quite dark. The outside door is open and* GRACE *stands in the doorway. The bright light inside pours into the darkness through the windows and the opened door, and beyond the door the cabinet containing the cigarettes and razors of the prisoners is clearly visible.*

LINTZ. Did everyone have enough to eat this morning?

All prisoners. Yes, sir.

Lintz. I didn't hear you, Two.

Two. Yes, sir.

Lintz. Your stomach all right, Two?

Two. Yes, sir.

Lintz. Front and center, Two. [Two *runs from his position in the ranks and stands in front of the formation.*] Give me twenty-five, Two. [Two *falls on his stomach and begins to do push-ups, but falls motionless after ten of them.*] On your feet, Two. Start running around the edge of the compound. [Two *begins running and continues as the scene progresses.*] Those who are not smoking fall out and form two ranks to your right. Move. [FOUR, SIX, *and* TEN *break from various points in the ranks and form near the right end of the compound.* GRACE *goes inside and opens the cabinet.*] Break, One.

ONE *runs toward the door. As he snaps his cap and passes through the door, he collides with* TEPPERMAN *who appears there. He falls, gets up, and stands at attention in front of* TEPPERMAN.

Tepperman [*long, loud, and all suffering*]. Woe. You touched me, you lousy insect. You actually came in contact with my clothing, infesting it with the disease of your stinking self. Now I will have to take a shower.

One [*terrified*]. I'm sorry, sir.

Tepperman [*punching the prisoner in the stomach*]. Never tell me you're sorry, boy. Move.

The prisoner runs through the door and stands at attention in front of the cabinet where GRACE *is standing.*

One. Sir, Prisoner Number One, sir.

GRACE *takes a pack of cigarettes from a box, taking one and throwing it at the prisoner. The prisoner catches it and remains at attention at the cabinet.*

Grace. Split.

The prisoner does an about-face and runs to the doorway, stopping and coming to attention. TEPPERMAN *is standing there.*

One. Sir, Prisoner Number One requests permission to cross the white line, sir.

Tepperman. Cross.

The prisoner returns to his position in ranks. As he arrives, THREE *automatically breaks from ranks and goes through the same process, getting one cigarette, and so on for the*

*others remaining in the larger formation. As the ceremony
ends, all are in possession of one cigarette.*

Lintz. Three, front and center. [THREE *breaks from the
ranks and stands in front of the formation.* LINTZ *takes a
lighter from his pocket, lights it, and places the lighter,
burning, through the fence.* THREE *lights his cigarette from
the outstretched hand of the guard, does an about-face, and
returns to the ranks.*] Parade rest. [*The men assume a stiff
at-ease position, smoking.* LINTZ *moves to the place where
the three men are standing at attention.*] Two, join the nonsmokers. [TWO, *who has been running around in circles,
joins the smaller group.*] Nonsmokers, at a half step, forward,
march. To the rear, march. To the rear, march. Squad, halt.
Parade rest.

*The smaller group responds to the commands, marching with
small steps in the limited area and ending up in the same
place, in the same position as those smoking.*

Tepperman. Smokers, put your cigarettes in your mouths.
Smokers, attention. [*The smoking group responds to the
commands and is at attention with cigarettes dangling from
their lips.* TEPPERMAN *walks through the ranks pausing occa-
sionally, taking a cigarette from the mouth of one, then another of the prisoners and crushing it beneath his foot. As
he does so, he informs the prisoner of the reason for it.*]
Talking at chow . . . Slow getting up this morning . . .
Too much time in the head . . . Sloppy rack . . . Bare
feet on the deck . . .

TEPPERMAN *walks through the outside door and disappears
within the Brig. The formation does not move.*

Lintz. Parade rest. Continue smoking. Nonsmokers, rejoin
the formation. [*The smaller formation rejoins the larger one,
assuming at once a motionless position of parade rest. The
only movements are the hands of the prisoners who are
smoking, moving from their lips to their sides, taking and
returning the cigarettes to and from their mouths.*] Put 'em
out. [*The prisoners smoking pinch the flame from the front*

of their cigarettes, rub them lightly in their palms to insure they are out, tear the paper from them, allowing the tobacco to fall to the ground, roll the paper in a ball, and drop it.] When I give you the word, I want you to get inside and break down for a shakedown. Is that clear?

All prisoners. Yes, sir.

Lintz. I can't hear you.

All prisoners. Yes, sir.

Lintz. You better sound off.

All prisoners. Yes, sir.

Lintz. Get inside.

The prisoners break off to the left, front rank first, and begin to disappear through the outside door in single file. Soon the outside compound is empty. LINTZ unloads his shotgun, opens the large double gates enough to step through them, locks and checks them, steps through the outside door, and closes it behind him. A flourish of activity can be seen through the windows.

Curtain.

SCENE 3

The inside of the Brig. The prisoners are standing at attention in their socks and underwear. THE WARDEN and all the guards are conducting a shakedown as explained in the Brig Regulations. As each prisoner is finished being searched, he puts on his clothes, takes his field jacket in his right hand, requests permission to cross the necessary white lines, and goes to his bunk. He then folds his field jacket, takes his cap from his pocket, and arranges them at the head of his bunk. He then takes his manual and begins reading it at attention

*in front of his bunk. As the guards search the prisoners, they
remark, striking and harassing their victims:*

Lintz. Change your skivvies tonight, Two. You smell like
a horse.

Two. Yes, sir.

Grace. You look like a horse, Six. Would you like to
change your face with mine?

Six. No, sir.

Grace. Are you telling me I'm ugly, Six?

Six. No, sir.

Grace. Would you like to kick my ass, Six?

Six. No, sir.

Grace. You're a liar, six.

The Warden [*punching a prisoner in the stomach*]. Four,
what were you talking about in chow this morning?

Four. Nothing, sir.

The Warden [*screaming*]. Nothing—— You can't talk
about nothing, Four. [*Hitting him again.*] See me at noon
chow, and you'll eat by the numbers.

Four. Yes, sir.

Tepperman. You're supposed to be standing at attention,
Eight, not getting ready to die. Are you going to die, Eight?

Eight. No, sir.

Tepperman. I wouldn't be too sure of that, Eight. [*The
search continues as the prisoners continue screaming out
their requests, and the guards continue saying, "Cross."
When all the prisoners are motionless in front of their bunks,
TEPPERMAN walks to the door of the head.*] All those who
want to make a head call on the white line.

All the prisoners cross and pass TEPPERMAN *as they enter
the head. Soon toilets are heard flushing and the prisoners
return to the compound one at a time. A bell rings, and
GRACE, who has just sat down at his desk, gets up and opens
the freedom door. Two men in pressed, starched dungarees
and polished boots enter the Brig armed with shotguns.
GRACE goes to his desk, takes two sheets of paper from it,
and hands one to each man. They greet him with a smile*

and: "How are you?" "How did it go last night?" *and* "We had a ball in town last night."

Grace. Everything's O.K. so far. [*And then to the last remark.*] Wait till tomorrow night when you guys are sweating it out in this joint. I'm going to tear me up some gook. [*He turns to the compound.*] Three, to the storeroom. Six, field jacket on, on the white line for work detail. [THREE *goes to the storeroom. The other man puts on his field jacket and moves to the white line. One of the men who just entered the Brig looks at his sheet of paper and goes out through the door that he entered.* GRACE *points to the white line in front of the freedom door.*] Work detail, get out here. [*The prisoner comes out of the compound and takes his position on the freedom door.*] Sound off, Six.

Six. Sir, Prisoner Number Six requests permission to cross the white line, sir.

Grace. Get out. [*The prisoner disappears through the door.*] Seven and Eight, field jackets on, on the white line for work detail. [*The two prisoners follow the instructions exactly as the man before them. The other guard with the shotgun studies his sheet of paper and goes outside.*] Work detail, get out here. [*The two prisoners come out of the compound and line up on the freedom door.*] Eight, break off to the storeroom for two shovels, move.

EIGHT *runs to the opposite end of the corridor next to the inside compound and comes to attention at the white line there.*

Eight. Sir, Prisoner Number Eight requests permission to cross the white line, sir.

Lintz [*standing there*]. Cross, Eight. [EIGHT *runs to the storeroom door and is handed two shovels by the storeroom man. He turns with them and is about to run for the formation awaiting him at the freedom door when he is stopped by* LINTZ's *command.*] Whoa, Eight. How long have you been a guest at my hotel?

Eight. Twelve days, sir.

Lintz. And you still don't know that you have to do a military about-face when you change direction?

Eight. Yes, I know it, sir.

Lintz [*walking toward the prisoner*]. What is this "I know it" business. You answer, "Yes, sir" or "No, sir" when you talk to me. Is that clear, maggot?

Eight. Yes, sir.

Lintz. Can't hear you.

Eight [*screaming*]. Yes, sir.

Lintz. You need some squaring away, maggot. [*Pause.*] Attention. [*The prisoner comes to a rigid position of attention, dropping the shovels on the floor. They clang loudly in the silence.*] Idiot. Breaking my shovels. I order you to die for such a crime. Die, idiot. [EIGHT *remains at a rigid position of attention. He begins weeping silently.*] Pick up the gear and move, maggot.

EIGHT *picks up both shovels and runs to the white line near the freedom door.*

Grace. Eight, you crossed my white line without asking me first. Tonight is your night, Eight. [GRACE *gets up and walks to the prisoner.*] Now give the other worm his shovel. [EIGHT *hands a shovel to the other prisoner.* GRACE *punches* EIGHT *in his stomach.*] Tonight is your night, Eight. [*Pause.*] Get out, maggots. [*Both prisoners disappear through the freedom door.*] Five, on the white line for work detail. [FIVE *puts on his field jacket, picks up his cap and runs to the white line.*] Five, get out here.

Five. Sir, Prisoner Number Five re——

Grace [*interrupting him*]. Cross. [*The prisoner comes to attention in front of the turnkey's desk.*] Did some little birdie tell you to put on your field jacket, my little field mouse?

Five. No, sir.

Grace. Then what the hell are you wearing it for? Do you think it's going to rain, Five?

Five. No, sir.

Grace. You go into the head, kneel in front of the toilet named two, and tell the toilet what you have done. Is that clear, Five?

Five. Yes, sir.

Grace. Do it.

FIVE *does a military about-face and runs to the door of the head. He comes to attention on the white line there.*

Five. Sir, Prisoner Number Five requests permission to cross the white line, sir.

Grace. Cross.

FIVE *goes inside the head. After a moment, a voice is heard from inside screaming loudly.*

Five. Sir, I put on my field jacket without being told.

Grace [*from his chair*]. Tell bowl two why, Five.

Five [*from inside*]. Sir, I put on my field jacket without being told because . . . [*Pause.*] I am a maggot.

Grace. Get out here, Five.

Five [*appearing in the door of the head*]. Sir——

Grace [*interrupting him*]. Cross the lines into the compound, take off your field jacket, put it on your bunk, cross the lines coming out, and get by the freedom door. [THE WARDEN *gets up from his desk, takes a shotgun from the office, and goes outside through the freedom door as* FIVE *does what he has been told.*] Sound off, Five.

Five. Sir, Prisoner Number Five requests permission to cross the white line, sir.

Grace. Cross. [*The prisoners leave through the door.* GRACE *gets up from his chair and walks to the freedom door. He slams it loudly and spins to face the other prisoners inside the compound who are still reading.*] One and Two get out here.

ONE *and* TWO *run to the white line.* ONE *arrives first and* TWO *falls in behind him.*

One. Sir, Prisoner Number One requests permission to cross the white line, sir.

Grace. Both of you better move and get over here. [*The*

two men come to attention abreast, in front of GRACE, *who is still at the door.* TEPPERMAN *who has remained leaning on the wall next to the head door comes over to them.*] Pfc. Tepperman is going to square you maggots away, is that clear?

Both prisoners. Yes, sir.

Grace. I can't hear you.

Both prisoners [*screaming*]. Yes, sir.

Tepperman. Louder, you motherless maggots.

Both prisoners [*bellowing*]. Yes, sir.

As TEPPERMAN *talks to the prisoners, he bends his head from side to side, almost touching their noses.*

Tepperman [*from one to the other*]. One, you dared come in contact with my body this morning. Now you must pay with a term of darkness. Two, by the time you get out of here, you will either have the strongest legs in the world, or you will be dead. Is that clear, Two?

Two. Yes, sir.

As TEPPERMAN *continues his folly, another scene is begun by* GRACE *and* LINTZ.

Grace. Pfc. Lintz, I think the maggots are out of shape. Put them through an exercise drill.

LINTZ *comes from the other side of the Brig. He enters the compound and stands inside the door with his arms folded.*

Lintz. I want all the racks moved to the far end of the compound on the double. Then I want you in two ranks, a body length apart facing me. [*The prisoners pick up all the double cots and move them into a corner one against the other, leaving a considerable space in the middle of the inside compound. They then occupy the space in two ranks, a body length from one another.*] All right, my bald children, down in the push-up position. By my count, one, two, one, two, one, two . . . [*He continues until the prisoners are all struggling and contorting to make the semblance of the exercise.*] On your feet. Sit-up position. By my count, one, two, one, two, one, two . . . [*Again he continues until they are exhausted.*] On your feet. Start running in place, and you better get those legs up. [*The prisoners are running in place, kicking their legs high in the air.*] On your bellies. On your feet. On your backs. You better get down when I tell you, maggots.

Without seeming to notice the other goings on, TEPPER-MAN *has gone on as follows during the exercise drill:*

Tepperman. There are bombs falling, One. Take cover on the spot. [ONE *falls to his knees and buries his head in his lap, covering it with his arms.*] Two, turn the G.I. can over on One to protect him from shrapnel. [Two *takes the cover from the garbage can next to the turnkey's desk, lays it on the floor, picks up the can, turns it over, and places it over the man on the floor. With* ONE *inside the inverted can,* Two *comes to attention.*] What is your first general order as a sentry, Two?

Two. Sir, to take charge of this post and all government property in view, sir.

Tepperman. Then you will pick up the G.I. can cover and run in a circle around One, who is armored government property, repeating your general order, and each third time around you will hit the can with the cover. Is that clear, Two?

Two. Yes, sir.

With Two *running around in circles screaming his general order and clanging the cover on the can, and the prisoners in the compound exercising to the commands of* LINTZ, TEPPERMAN *and* GRACE *begin laughing out loud.*

Curtain.

ACT TWO

SCENE 1

Inside the Brig. All prisoners are in a single line abreast standing at attention facing the chicken wire, inches from it, in the corridor. They each hold a field jacket in their left hand and a cap in their right hand. Their shoelaces are opened and their dungaree jackets are outside their trousers and also opened. Their trousers are unbuttoned, but this is not visible in their present position.

THE WARDEN. I thought noon chow was excellent today, kiddies. Do you think you could find such fine chow anywhere else outside of my Marine Corps?

All prisoners. No, sir.

The Warden. You bet your life you couldn't. Are you all broken down for a frisk?

All prisoners. Yes, sir.

All the personnel of the Brig are present and standing with THE WARDEN. *As he continues talking, he walks up the corridor, behind the prisoners, stationing a guard every five feet.*

The Warden. I understand that tonight is your night, Eight. Tell us why.

Eight [from the line, without moving]. Sir, it is my night because I dropped the shovels, sir.

The Warden. Whose shovels, Eight?

Eight. Your shovels, sir.

As THE WARDEN *is talking, he taps a prisoner on the shoulder and jumps back. The prisoner lifts his hat and his right leg, snaps the hat on his thigh, throws his legs out behind him, and grips the wire with outstretched arms high and hard. Thus the frisk of the prisoners begins.* THE WARDEN *then feels all the clothing of the prisoner down into his open*

63

shoes, hitting the prisoner on the leg as he finishes. The prisoner jumps up erect and does an about-face, holding his field jacket by the shoulders with both hands in front of him. THE WARDEN *searches the jacket and then says,* "Get out." *The prisoner runs to the white line in the rear of the corridor and requests permission to cross it.* THE WARDEN *grants it and the prisoner runs to the door of the compound, stops, and requests permission again to cross the white line.*

The Warden. Cross. All prisoners after they have been frisked will go to the inside compound, fold their field jackets on their racks, and fall in on the white line to make a head call. [*The other guards begin frisking the prisoners in silence, except for the word* "Cross," *which is spoken to the prisoners requesting to cross the line into the compound. As the line inside the compound begins to grow,* THE WARDEN *walks to the door of the compound.*] Sound off.

Eight [*at the front of the line*]. Sir, Prisoner Number Eight requests permission to cross the white line, sir.

The Warden. All prisoners cross all the white lines into and out of the head and get in front of your racks with your manuals.

The last of the men being frisked requests permission to cross into the compound, make their head call, and soon all is quiet in the Brig. THE WARDEN *goes to his desk,* LINTZ *to Post One,* GRACE *to his desk, and* TEPPERMAN *to Post Two.*

Tepperman. Button up, maggots. [*The prisoners whose clothing is still opened tie their shoelaces, button and tuck in their dungarees, fasten their belts, and return to their manuals.*] There will be no working parties this afternoon because this Brig looks like a garbage dump, and I think it's about time we had a little field day. Any objections, Two?

Two. No, sir.

TEPPERMAN *enters the compound and walks to* PRISONER NUMBER TWO.

Tepperman. I don't think you know what a field day is, do you, Two?

Two. Yes, sir.

Tepperman. Well then, tell us what it is. You are a new louse in my house and I know you never saw us have a field day so you just tell us what it is.

Two. It is a thorough cleaning of the living quarters, sir.

Tepperman [*punching* Two *in the stomach*]. It is a sterilization of the Brig, Two. From now on you don't invent your own definitions, you memorize ours. Is that clear, Two?

Two. Yes, sir.

Lintz. Get over here to the storeroom, Three.

THREE *runs to the storeroom.* THE WARDEN *rises from his desk, walks up the corridor, enters the compound, and walks up and down the aisle between the racks talking.*

The Warden. Those of you who have been in my house for more than a week are familiar with the field day. Those who are not will benefit by what I say. You will be told what to do only once, and you'd better understand the orders you are given and carry them out exactly as they are given you, because I like to live in a clean house. When you are finished, everything will look exactly as it does now, but it will be clean. If the field day is successful, you will be permitted to write letters for one-half hour after dinner this evening. Is that clear, children?

All prisoners. Yes, sir.

The Warden. Carry on, Pfc. Tepperman.

Tepperman. One and Two, tear down all racks, fold all blankets, and place them under the stripped pillows. Put all dirty linen into four separate sheets, go to the storeroom, draw new linen, and make up all the racks—and they better be tight. Four and Five, to the storeroom and draw scrub brushes. I want to see you scrubbers on the deck putting some elbow grease into it. You will get on your knees and start scrubbing at the head door, moving to the other end of the Brig on my command. Six, to the storeroom for a squeegee. You will fall in behind the scrubbers and keep the soapy water in front of them, and it better be dry in back of you.

Seven, bucket man. You will go to the storeroom and draw four boxes of soap flakes. You will then take one G.I. can next to the turnkey's desk into the head and put one box of soap in it at a time, filling it with hot water from the shower, and throwing it across the front of the line of scrubbers. When the four boxes of soap have been used up, you will begin throwing clear hot water in front of the squeegee until I tell you to stop. Then you will secure the G.I. can in the head, go to the storeroom, draw a swab and bucket, and join the swabbers. Eight and Nine, to the storeroom for swabs and buckets. You maggots will fall in behind the squeegee and swab up all the soap and water. When your bucket is three-quarters full of water, you will go into the head and empty it down the shower drain. And when we are finished that deck had better be dry. Ten, to the storeroom for clean rags and a bucket. You will wash the windows. Draw cold water from the head and make all the glass in this house sparkle. Let's get hot. [*As* TEPPERMAN *speaks, the Brig becomes once again a beehive of activity. All the prisoners follow their instructions,* GRACE *and* THE WARDEN *stand on top of their desks,* LINTZ *enters the compound and sits on a top bunk that has already been undressed, and* TEPPERMAN *goes into the head. Water from the large garbage can and soapsuds veritably flood the deck, with those on their knees scrubbing and getting soaking wet. The squeegee man fights desperately to keep the soap forward of the scrubbers, and the swabbers dry up the water as quickly as possible, rinsing the water in their buckets. The window washer wipes the windows one at a time with a wet rag and then rubs them dry feverishly, for what seems much longer than is necessary, and the guards from their safe and dry positions issue many warnings and instructions.* TEPPERMAN *stands inside the head door.*] Scrubbers, move forward three feet. Squeegee detail, get hot behind them. Swabbers stand by. Bucket man, I better see more soap and water on this deck.

GRACE *throws his hands over his head, standing straddle-legged on his desk.*

Grace. Let me hear the music of those brushes. Elbow grease, my children, elbow grease. What's the matter, Four? I can't hear your brush. It must sing in the suds, Four, is that clear?

Four [his arm going like a windmill]. Yes, sir.

Lintz. I want all these racks made up and in place by the time the scrubbers arrive. Is that clear, rack detail?

Rack detail. Yes, sir.

Tepperman. That's enough water, bucket man. Secure the can in the shower and draw your swab and bucket. Scrubbers, up three more feet. Swab detail, get hot.

The Warden. Rub your arms off, kiddies. Are you happy, window detail?

Window detail. Yes, sir.

The Warden. They are our windows you are washing, is that clear?

Window detail. Yes, sir.

Tepperman. Scrubbers, you will now move forward one yard on the command "move," and every time I say "move" in the future. When we get to the compound wire, Five will do the corridor. Four will enter the compound. Move.

Lintz. These racks better be ready when the scrubbers arrive.

Tepperman. Move.

Grace. You are next to the freedom door, Four. Are you going to make a break for it?

Four. No, sir.

The Warden. I can't hear you, Four.

Four. No, sir.

Warden. Eight, as you swab you will sing one chorus of my favorite song. When Eight is finished, we will have one chorus from Nine. When Nine is finished, we will have one chorus from Two. Begin, Eight.

EIGHT *begins the* "Marine Corps Hymn." *The field day goes on uninterruptedly as the other two prisoners each render their chorus in turn.*

Tepperman. Move.

Lintz. Move. Are all the racks finished?

Rack detail [*working feverishly tightening the blankets*]. Yes, sir.

LINTZ *walks out of the compound and past the scrubbers and others behind them.* TEPPERMAN *comes out of the head and walks into the compound, punching* LINTZ *lightly on the arm as they pass each other.*

Lintz. Rack detail, in two ranks on me.

Both men stop tightening the racks, request permission to cross out of the compound, TEPPERMAN *grants it, and they fall in facing* LINTZ *behind the working group.*

Tepperman. Move, Five in the corridor, Four in the compound.

LINTZ *drills the two men in the confines of Post Two.*

Lintz. Rack detail, at a half step, forward march, to the rear march, left flank march . . . [*He continues to call commands.*]

The Warden. As you are working, prisoners sound off.

All the prisoners, one at a time, call out their numbers in the following manner: "Sir, Prisoner Number One, sir," "Sir, Prisoner Number Two, sir." *And so on through* TEN.

Tepperman. Move. You maggots are falling behind schedule. You better bear into those brushes.

The Warden. Window detail, are the windows secure?

Window detail. Yes, sir.

The Warden. Empty your water in the shower, secure your gear in the storeroom, and join the marchers.

LINTZ *halts the formation again, awaits the arrival of the window washer, and begins drilling once more.*

Tepperman. Move slowly to the wire. When Four has reached the far end of the compound, he will join Five in Post One, moving on my command. Seven, you will follow

them drying up the mess they make on the way. Is that clear?
All involved. Yes, sir.

FOUR *reaches the wire, gets up, and runs around the wire barrier to Post Two, returning to his knees outside the wire on the other end of the Brig.* SEVEN *follows swabbing up the water that drips from his soaking pants. The squeegee man pushes the water through the wire and the scrubbing begins again.*

The Warden. It had better be white under my desk.

Tepperman. Move, squeegee, join the scrubbers outside the compound. [*The procession continues until the scrubbers reach the front wall of the Brig.*] Secure the scrub brushes and join the formation. [*The scrubbers hand their brushes to the storeroom man.* LINTZ *halts the marchers until they are joined by the scrubbers, then begins again.* THE WARDEN *climbs down from his desk and opens the large double doors in front of the Brig. The man with the squeegee then pushes the water outside, and the swabbers finish drying the deck.*] Secure all the gear, and join the formation. Ten, get in the head and clean and dry the G.I. can, then put it back where it belongs.

Soon all the prisoners are drilling in the tiny space between the head and the compound. GRACE *waves to* LINTZ *and* LINTZ *stops the drill. They are all at attention facing the compound. All the guards and* THE WARDEN *come to Post Two.*

The Warden. What did you think of the field day, Two?
Two. Sir, it was a thorough field day, sir.
The Warden. All prisoners in the compound at attention with their manuals.

THE WARDEN *returns to his desk,* TEPPERMAN *sits on the edge of the turnkey's desk,* LINTZ *goes to Post One, and the prisoners scramble into the compound and are soon motionless in front of their racks.*

Curtain.

SCENE 2

The prisoners are marching in place in front of their racks.
Tepperman *is calling cadence, sitting on* Grace's *desk.*

Tepperman. Un doo, ree, ree der lef doo ree, ree der lef.
Yer mother was there when you left.
　　Prisoners. Yer right.
　　Tepperman. Yer father was there when you left.
　　Prisoners. Yer right.
　　Tepperman. Sound off.
　　Prisoners. One, two.
　　Tepperman. Sound off.
　　Prisoners. Three, four.
　　Tepperman. Ad'ance count.
　　Prisoners. One, two, three, four, one, two . . . [*Pause.*]
three, four.
　　Tepperman. Ris'ners h'lt. P'rade rest.

The prisoners stop marching and come to a stiff at-ease posi-
tion.

　　Grace. Three, Five is getting out. As senior man in my
house, you know what to do. Do it.

Five *smiles openly.* Tepperman *enters the compound and*
punches him in the stomach. The smile disappears.

　　Tepperman. You are not out yet, Five. You will not laugh
unless I tell you to laugh. Is that clear, Five?
　　Five. Yes, sir.

Tepperman *returns to the desk.* Three *requests permission*
to cross the lines to and from the storeroom and returns with
a seabag that appears about three-quarters full. He goes to
the box of Five *and empties its contents neatly into the bag.*
Grace *goes to the cabinet and removes* Five's *razor and*
cigarettes. Three *requests permission to cross to the freedom*

door and back, leaving the bag beside it. GRACE *places the razor and cigarettes in the bag, closes it, and goes back to his desk. The bell rings:* TEPPERMAN *opens the door, sticks his head out, and yells,* "Stand by." *He comes back and sits on the desk.*

Grace. Five, get out here. Bring your towel and laundry bag. [FIVE *goes to the rear of his bunk, takes his towel and laundry bag, requests permission to cross the line inside the compound, and stands in front of* GRACE's *desk.* GRACE *smiles.*] Well, you better sound off, Five.

Five. Sir, Prisoner Number Five reporting as ordered, sir.

Tepperman. What are your orders, Five?

Five. To report to the turnkey's desk, sir.

Grace. How long have you been in my house, Five?

Five. Twenty-five days, sir.

Tepperman. What was your sentence, Five.

Five. Thirty days, sir.

Grace. Do you know why five days have been taken off your sentence, Five?

Tepperman. Well, do you, Five?

Five. Yes, sir, for good conduct, sir.

Grace. Prisoners, attention. Prisoners, left face. [*The prisoners come to attention and do the facing movement as commanded so they are facing the turnkey.*] Pick up your seabag, and get on the freedom line, Five. [FIVE *does an about-face, picks up his seabag, puts it on his shoulder, and stands on the line opposite the freedom door.*] Sound off, Five.

Five [*triumphantly*]. Sir, Prisoner Number Five requests permission to cross the white line, sir.

The Warden [*from his desk*]. I can't hear you.

Five [*with gusto*]. Sir, Prisoner Number Five requests permission to cross the white line, sir.

Lintz [*from the corridor*]. I can't hear you.

Five [*bellowing*]. Sir, Prisoner Number Five requests permission to cross the white line, sir.

TEPPERMAN *gets up chuckling. He goes to the door and puts his nose against* FIVE's *forehead.*

Tepperman. One more time, Five, just one more time.

Five. Sir, Prisoner Number——

Tepperman [*interrupting him*]. Get out, get out of my house.

FIVE *disappears through the door and* TEPPERMAN *slams it shut.*

Grace. Prisoners, right face.

Tepperman. Back to your manuals, and someday, if you are good maggots who clean under their short hairs every day, you may be free. [*All prisoners except* SIX *pick up their books and start reading.* SIX *emits a terrifying scream and falls to his knees. The other prisoners near him jump with fright. All give him a probing glance. Then everyone returns to his reading.* TEPPERMAN *runs into the compound, billy club in hand, and stands over the prisoner, who has buried his head in his hands and is weeping.*] On your feet, Six.

Six [*looking up*]. I am thirty-four years old. For God's sake, let me out of this madhouse. I'm not one of these damned kids. I can't stand it any more.

Tepperman. I told you to get on your feet, Six.

SIX *begins to whine and tremble. He lunges from the floor at* TEPPERMAN, *who deftly steps aside and brings his weapon down on the side of the prisoner's face. At this,* GRACE *and* LINTZ *run into the compound.* THE WARDEN *runs from his desk and locks the door to the sleeping area. The prisoner fights savagely with the three guards screaming continually, "Let me out of here." Eventually he is subdued and taken to solitary cell one at the front of the Brig. He can be heard from within the cell, as* THE WARDEN *observes him.*

Six. Sixteen years I give to this rotten outfit and they throw me in an asylum. Somebody's got to listen to me. It's all wrong. Two weeks in this place and already I'm out of my mind. Let me out of here.

THE WARDEN *shakes his head from side to side and goes into the Brig officer's office. He comes out a few minutes later.*

The Warden [*to* LINTZ]. They're coming for him.

LINTZ *shakes his head affirmatively.*

Tepperman. Anybody else who wants to crack up, do it now, so that when they come for him, you can keep him company.

The prisoners continue reading. GRACE *goes into the compound and walks up and down the aisle studying the faces of the prisoners as they read.*

Grace. It would be a good night for you to crack up, Eight, because this is your night.

Tepperman. Are you going to crack up, Eight?

Eight [*putting his book by his side*]. No, sir. [*He does not resume reading.*]

Lintz. You must be out of your mind to have dropped my shovels, isn't that so, Eight?

Grace. Back to your book, Eight.

Six [*from his cell*]. My name is not Six. It's James Turner. Let me out of here.

The Warden. Three, take Six's gear to the storeroom and put it in his seabag. Then put his seabag by the freedom door.

THREE *does as he is told, requesting permission to cross the lines in the process and receiving it. The bell rings.* GRACE *comes out of the compound and opens the door. Two men in white coats and trousers carrying a stretcher and a strait jacket enter and are led to the cell of* SIX. *They enter it.*

Six. What the hell is going on here? Leave me alone.

Grace. Just relax, James Turner. You are getting out of here.

The two men come out of the cell carrying a stretcher with the prisoner on it secured to the stretcher in the strait jacket. The prisoner babbles as they carry him off.

Six. Thank God, I'm getting out of here. I really don't believe it.

GRACE *carries his seabag outside and returns, slamming the door behind him.*

Tepperman. Secure the reading material; field jackets on; on the line for evening chow. [*As the prisoners put on their jackets and line up by the door of the compound,* THE WARDEN, GRACE, *and* LINTZ *take shotguns from the Brig officer's office, open the outside door, and go out.* TEPPER-MAN *stands at the head door.*] Get outside.

The prisoners file through the outside door in a trot, snapping their hats on an uplifted thigh as they go through it. TEPPER-MAN *looks at his watch and goes through the door, closing it behind him. The Brig is once more empty and silent.*

Curtain.

SCENE 3

The prisoners are seated at the long table writing letters. Some do not fit at the table so they are seated on the floor with their pencils, writing pads, and envelopes. TEPPERMAN *walks out of the head and sits on* GRACE's *desk. They begin to whisper to each other.* LINTZ *is leaning on* THE WARDEN's *desk, and they too are holding an inaudible conversation. The prisoners begin addressing envelopes, folding their let-ters, and putting them inside the envelopes.*

GRACE. Secure the writing gear and get in front of your racks for collection.

The prisoners place their equipment in their boxes and fall in at attention in front of their bunks. GRACE *enters the compound and collects the letters from the hands of the prisoners.*

The Warden. Two, what is the rule for letter-writing?

Two. Sir, the rule is that the letter shall not exceed the length of one side of a page.

Tepperman. How do you know that, Two?

Two. Sir, because you explained it to me before the letter-writing period, sir.

The Warden. When I read these letters, I better not find any sealed envelopes or any letters containing material against my Marine Corps. Is that clear, kiddies?

All prisoners. Yes, sir.

The bell rings. TEPPERMAN *opens the freedom door, steps back quickly, leaving the door ajar.*

Tepperman [*bellowing*]. You better get in here on the double, maggot. Put those seabags on your shoulders and face the wall to your right. [*A Marine enters in starched dungarees with the collar open, his hat on, and a seabag in each hand. He is obviously terrified. He places a seabag on each shoulder, turns and faces the wall, and soon begins shaking from the weight his arms and shoulders are supporting.* TEPPERMAN *sticks his head out the door, saying,* "That will be all, Sentry," *slams the door and walks over to the new prisoner. He takes off the prisoner's cap and slams it down on the floor in front of him. The man does not budge.*] Next time you wear a hat in my house, I will chop your head off. Is that very clear?

The prisoner [*weakly*]. Yes, sir.

Tepperman [*punching the man in the side*]. When you speak in this place, you speak loud and clear. Is that very clear?

The prisoner [*dropping one seabag*]. Yes, sir.

Tepperman [*punching him again*]. Yes, sir, you better sound off boy 'cause I can't hear you.

Prisoner [*quickly picking up the seabag*]. Yes, sir.

Grace [*from his desk*]. About face. [*There is no response from the prisoner.* GRACE *jumps from his desk and screams in the prisoner's ear.*] About face. [*The prisoner responds, turning around.*] When you hear a command in my house, you better snap to. Your sniveling mouse eyes will be black if you ever do that again. Is that clear, maggot?

The prisoner. Yes, sir.

Tepperman. Louder.

The prisoner. Yes, sir.

Grace. Forward march. [*The prisoner walks to the other wall of the Brig. As he reaches it:*] Right flank, march.

The prisoner marches down the corridor.

Tepperman. Ree pree der lef reet left. Pick him up, Lintz.

Lintz. Left reet left ree der left. [*The prisoner marches past the white line at the end of the corridor. Two steps over the line, Lintz gives a command.*] Right flank, march. 'Ris'ner, h'lt. Right face.

The prisoner ends his march at attention in front of THE WARDEN'*s desk.*

The Warden. Three, get out here. [*The new prisoner shakes as* THE WARDEN *speaks. Soon* THREE *is standing next to him at the desk.*] You better stand still, boy. Drop those bags on the floor. Three, get the necessary gear out of those bags in the storeroom and secure the rest. [THREE *picks up the bags and disappears with them into the storeroom.*] Get your hat, maggot. [*The prisoner does not move.* THE WARDEN *leaps from his desk, pushing the prisoner with tremendous force. The prisoner stumbles across the room, falling down, getting up again, running to* THE WARDEN, *and coming to attention in front of him.* THE WARDEN *smiles.*] I thought you were going to swing at me, boy. I would have loved that. [*His face becomes cross.*] Did you hear me tell you to get your hat?

The prisoner. Yes, sir.

The Warden. Do you know where it is?

The prisoner. Yes, sir.

The Warden. Then what the hell are you doing standing

here like a dead worm? Get the hell out of here; get your hat and report back to me. [*The prisoner starts running to retrieve his cap.*] Get back here right away, maggot. [*The prisoner turns and comes back.* THE WARDEN *punches him in the stomach.*] When you are dismissed from anyone's company around here, you do a military about-face. Is that clear?

The prisoner. Yes, sir.

The Warden. Split.

The prisoner does an about-face, runs up the corridor, passes the line at the end of it, and bends over to pick up his cap. As he bends over, TEPPERMAN *runs over to him and grasps the back of his neck.*

Tepperman. Now you stay bent down, boy, and follow my hand as it leads you, or I'll break your neck. [TEPPERMAN *leads the prisoner, who is almost doubled over, to the line at the end of the corridor.*] Do you see that line, maggot.

The prisoner. Yes, sir.

Tepperman. Well, just to make sure, you get down on your knees and put your nose on it. [*The prisoner does as he is told.*] Whenever you see one of those lines in my house, you will stop and come to attention. Then you will sound off: "Sir, Prisoner Number—whatever number you are given— requests permission to cross the white line, sir." Is that clear?

The prisoner. Yes, sir.

Tepperman. It had better be. [*Pause.*] Get out of here.

The prisoner stands up, does an about-face, and runs to the white line at the other end of the corridor with his hat in his hand. He stops and comes to attention, but does not murmur a word. THE WARDEN *sits looking at him for a moment.*

The Warden. Well?

The prisoner. Sir, I have no number, sir.

The Warden. Your number is Five, maggot.

Five. Sir, Prisoner Number Five requests permission to cross the white line, please.

The Warden. "Please"! Who the hell told you to say "please"? What do you think this is, a finishing school?

Five. Sir, Prisoner Number Five requests permission to cross the white line, sir.

The Warden. Cross. [FIVE *comes to attention in front of* THE WARDEN's *desk.*] When you are summoned in my house, you say, "Sir, Prisoner Number Five reporting as ordered, sir."

Five. Sir, Prisoner Number Five reporting as ordered, sir.

The Warden. What are your orders?

Five. To come to your desk with my hat, sir.

THREE *comes out of the storeroom with all the clothing, towels, laundry bag, cigarettes, razor, blades, and manual of the prisoner. He stands in front of the desk and hands the things to the new* FIVE.

The Warden. Five, and that is your name from now on, this is the one and only time that you will be permitted to talk to anyone in this Brig. Three will explain our procedure to you and you may ask him questions. After that, if you talk, you will need new teeth. Follow him to the compound.

The two prisoners cross into the compound and then a pantomime ensues. They are talking to each other, but in such low tones that it is incomprehensible. THREE *starts folding clothes and putting them in the box marked "Five." There is a shaking of heads and a completion of the task. Then the placing of the laundry bag and towel, identification of bunk, folding of field jacket, indicating the place for the hat and manual, more shaking of heads, and the close scrutiny of* TEPPERMAN, *who has just entered the compound.*

Three. Sir, the cigarette, razor, and blades are on the rack, sir.

TEPPERMAN *picks up the articles from the bunk of* FIVE *and places them inside the cabinet outside the compound.*

Tepperman. Front of your racks, Three and Five. Everybody strip down for a shower and get on the line in numerical order. [*The prisoners strip to their boots and underwear, take their towels from the back of their racks, dropping their clothes there, take soap and clean underwear, toothbrushes*

*and toothpaste from their boxes, and fall in on the line by
the door of the compound. When they are all lined up,*
TEPPERMAN *speaks.*] First five out get here. [GRACE *goes to
the cabinet and opens it. The prisoners line up in front of
him. Each prisoner carries all his equipment in his left hand,
and the five men in front of* GRACE *have their hands ex-
tended high in the air. He places a razor in each of their
empty right hands. They move to the door of the head with
their hands still high over their heads, are granted permission
to cross by* TEPPERMAN, *and disappear inside with* TEPPER-
MAN *following them.* LINTZ *comes from the other end of the
Brig and stands near the door to the compound. The showers
are heard running, toilets flushing, sinks filling, and* TEPPER-
MAN'S *voice from within.*] You better move, maggots, you're
not in here on a health cure. Get those whiskers off, Two.
You better get that razor up in the air, Two. Do you want
to kill me or one of the idiots you live with? Send me five
more, Lintz.

Lintz. Next five.

*The next five prisoners repeat the same process as those who
preceded them, scrutinized carefully by* LINTZ *and* GRACE.
The second man in line speaks.

Ten. Sir, Prisoner Number Ten requests a change of blades,
sir.

GRACE *changes the blade in his razor before handing it to
him.* LINTZ *grants them permission to cross into the head
as the first five are given permission to come out. They are
clothed in clean underwear streaked with water, and it is
obvious that they had little time to dry themselves. Their
razors are taken from their uplifted hands by* GRACE, *and as
this is done, they take their towels in their right hands; as
they cross into the compound, the towels are snapped loudly.
They return their bathing tools to their proper places, go to
their racks, and, in their underwear, begin reading.* TEPPER-
MAN *comes out of the head, and* LINTZ *goes into the compound.*

Lintz. Manuals away.

Tepperman. Get all the gear off your racks and get them ready for habitation. [*The prisoners take all their paraphernalia from the heads of their bunks and place it on the floor with their clothing. They then resume a position of attention in front of their bunks.* GRACE *flicks a switch beside his head and all the lights go out except the ones in the head. The light casts itself across the Brig, making the prisoners appear as shadows.*] Sound off.

One. Sir, Prisoner Number One, sir.

The rest of the prisoners answer in the same way, one at a time, using their own numbers.

Tepperman. Get in.

The prisoners jump in their bunks, leaving their shoes on the floor.

Grace. Get out.

The prisoners jump from their bunks into their shoes and come to attention again.

Lintz. Get in.

The prisoners jump in once more.

The Warden. Are all my children asleep?

All prisoners. Yes, sir.

GRACE *flicks another switch and the stage is black.*

Curtain.

DIRECTING *THE BRIG*

DIRECTING *THE BRIG*

The dramatic and psychological situations have passed here into the very sign language of the combat, which is a function of the mystic athletic play of bodies and the undulatory use of the stage, whose enormous spiral reveals itself in one perspective after another.

The warriors enter the mental forest rocking with fear, over-whelmed by a great shudder. It is more than a physical tempest, it is a spiritual concussion that is signified in the general trem-bling of their limbs and their rolling eyes. The sonorous pulsa-tion of their bristling heads is at times excruciating and the music sways behind them and at the same time sustains an unimaginable space into which real pebbles finally roll.

—Antonin Artaud *

THE BRIG IS A STRUCTURE. The precision of the description of this structure is the key to *The Brig.*

The Immovable Structure is the villain. Whether that structure calls itself a prison or a school or a factory or a family or a government or The World As It Is. That struc-ture asks each man what he can do for it, not what it can do for him, and for those who do not do for it, there is the pain of death or imprisonment, or social degradation, or the loss of animal rights.

The men placed inside the structure are intended to be-come part of this structure, and the beauty and terror of *The Brig* is seeing how it succeeds and how it fails in in-corporating those whom it has imprisoned into its own cor-poreal being.

Reading the minutiae of description with which Kenneth Brown prefaces his play, I already felt that beauty and that terror in the rigor of the detail. A long time ago Kenneth Brown found himself in such a room and he noted with precision the proportions of the wire enclosure, the turnkey's desk, the Warden's post, and the white lines on the deck.

* This quotation and the other references to Artaud are from *The Theatre and Its Double* by Antonin Artaud, translated by M. C. Richards, published by Grove Press.

And as he stood there for thirty days at attention with his eyes in *The Guidebook for Marines*, he realized that what was happening to him was significant. Here in the darkness under the bright overhead light there lay exposed the open wound of violence.

Though the social structure begins by framing the noblest laws and the loftiest ordinances that "the great of the earth" have devised, in the end it comes to this: breach that lofty law and they take you to a prison cell and shut your human body off from human warmth. Ultimately the law is enforced by the unfeeling guard punching his fellow man hard in the belly.

And Kenneth Brown saw it and he experienced it and he wrote it down when he got out of it.

Reading the disembodied commands of *The Brig*, the numbered shouts that evoke the machine but remain transcendentally human outcries, I heard clearly in my ears the familiar metal scraping prison sounds and the stamp of the booted foot on concrete. These sounds will haunt me forever as they will haunt all of us who have been prisoners. The month that I spent in the Women's House of Detention was not only instructive, but it enables me to count myself as always among the prisoners. I needed to loosen my subjective response.

Four masterworks came to my mind after reading Brown's play. The work of three great men of the modern theatre, a Russian, a Frenchman, and a German, the fourth of collective and ancient authorship; all served as instruction on how to proceed.

The Work of Meyerhold

His tormented specter appeared. I said to him: "Alas, you called your whole life a 'search for a style,' pursuing that search through honor and disgrace. Now, at last, I have found the play in which the actor is biologically and mechanically enmeshed inside the construction of wires and white lines."

He was rehearsing the *Death of Tintagal* when the Revolution burst forth and poured him into the street to do battle on the stages of the Revolution. He set up troupes that brought the political theatre to the railroad stations, the factories, the barricades, to the fronts of the Revolution. And afterward, installed in his state-subsidized theatre, he went on with his search. He came to believe that only complex technical structures overpowering the actor could express the real scenery of his times.

The Constructivist demands a setting which *is* the action. Therefore, Meyerhold began to regulate the actor's movements until his actors complained that they were being treated like puppets. In a public attack his theatre was dubbed "hostile to the people."

He tried puppets and failed. When he spoke of his theory of bio-mechanics as "the organization and geometrization of movement, based on deep study of the human body," he knew that something psychophysical was at stake; that the way back to the sensibilities of the spectator must be through referring again to the human body standing there trapped before him. The actor is not disembodied of his soul, but is full with it and controls it to fill out the dramatic and metaphysical construction.

In *The Brig* each actor feels his total creativity when the external form of his action is so inhibited and his single repeated phrase is so limiting that his whole discarnate soul quivers in his face and body and the performances become filled with invention and full of mystery. Each actor has his mystery and his trip.

The Brig is a Constructivist play. The construction of the set dictates and directs the action by the power of its vectors and its centers of gravity. It was designed by the architects of ancient military prisons, Masonic craftsmen of dungeons and towers. From these fearsome structures the utility of minimal construction and maximum security is in direct descent.

Kenneth Brown vividly recollected the actuality as adapted

by the U.S. Marines at the foot of Mount Fuji in 1957. Only Beck's ingenious sense of proportion was needed to create a Constructivist stage.

In *The Brig*, Vsevolod Emilyevich, without damaging the actor's powers, but rather bearing them up, the structure enforces that rhythmic discipline of the actor's body, which you called "bio-mechanics."

THE WORK OF ARTAUD

To Artaud, my madman muse, never absent from my dreams, I speak in a private language. He it was who demanded of the actor the great athletic feats: the meaningless gestures broken off into dances of pain and insanity; who cried out in his crazy-house cell for a theatre so violent that no man who experienced it would ever stomach violence again. He said: "I defy any spectator to whom such violent scenes will have transferred their blood—the violence of blood having been placed at the service of the violence of the thought—I defy that spectator to give himself up, once outside the theatre, to ideas of war, riot, and blatant murder."

Artaud asks for a theatre in which the actors are victims burned at the stake "signaling through the flames"; in which "physical obsession of muscles quivering with affectivity, is equivalent, as in the play of breaths, to unleashing this affectivity in full force, giving it a mute but profound range of extraordinary violence"; in which "The overlapping of images and movements will culminate, through the collusion of objects, silences, shouts, and rhythms, or in a genuinely physical language with signs, not words, as its root."

O Antonin fierce and demanding, in *The Brig* I have seen the actor tax his body to that abstract athletic splendor where he looms on the precarious edge of the abyss of soullessness.

THE WORK OF PISCATOR

But Piscator was my teacher, so I must apply stricter rules to meet his standards. Besides, he is no historical dream figure. Even now in the Divided City he works in the old Berliner Volksbühne to create a theatre as potent politically as that which, across the bloodstained wall, is the great monument to his old friend and colleague, Bertolt Brecht.

Where Artaud cries out for Madness, Piscator advocates Reason, Clarity, and Communication. He said once in class, "We have gone back to what we can see, because although we know that other things exist, that which we can see is organizable."

Brecht writes of Piscator:

His experiments caused, above all, complete chaos in the theatre. If the stage was transformed into a machine shop, then the auditorium was transformed into an assembly hall. For Piscator the theatre was a parliament, the public a legislative body. To this parliament was presented in plastic terms important, decision-demanding, public affairs. In place of an address by a member of parliament concerning certain untenable social conditions, there appeared an artistic reproduction of the situation. Piscator's theatre wanted to wrest from the spectators a practical resolve to take an active hold on life.

My dear Mr. Piscator: once in a class you described the totally effective revolutionary play. My class notes tell me you called it *Die Stimme von Portugal*. You described how the performer sang the last phrases of a rousing chorus on freedom and how the people went singing out of the theatre and freed their native land from the oppressor. I have not yet found a play that can move the spectator to such commitment. But I have found a play so valid that when it was closed by the state because the theatre could not meet its financial obligations, the actors, the author, the stage hands, the box-office workers, the stage manager, the house manager, and the technicians were joined by some members of the audience in volunteering to be arrested on the stage with us rather than leave without protesting that this play should not continue to speak.

In our indictment we are charged with shouting from the windows, "Storm the barricades!"

THE WORK OF *The Guidebook for Marines*

The great men, or so the historians call them, having lost the names of the men who invented the wheel and alphabet, have spent their powers in the study of combat. Caesar, and the Pharaohs, and before them the tribal kings, and after them the Napoleons in their many uniforms and national characteristics have all given over the fruits of their genius to the battlefield. Strategy has come to be regarded as fit exercise for the best in human consciousness.

But before the battle, the soldier must be trained. Get them young. Get them while they are pliable to the process of conforming them to the soldierly shape.

Men studied how to train the young to kill before they trained them to build, or to write, or to work the land. Only singing and dancing came before that ancient skill. Before the worst, only the best was known. First the lute, then the spear. And after the singing, the arrows.

The line of learning can be traced, and, were I a scholar, I might trace how some writer in hieroglyphics first formulated the about face, or at what point in history the cadence count was developed out of the old war cries, and how the particular shininess of the uniform was discovered to heighten the will to kill.

I saw that what I confronted in this fearsome book was the compendium of a time-honored study. Nothing has been more carefully formulated than the manuals of war. When I read *The Guidebook for Marines* I said this book is one of the great books and set it beside the Holy Writ (which has much study of strategy in it) and *The Zohar* (which attributes even to the heavenly orders the terminology of the military discipline).

The Marine Corps manual represents the acme of the venerable line of study manuals designed to teach men to kill and function in the battle situation. The preparation of men for this ordeal, being so innately unnatural to human affection and so innately natural to the human animal, exploits the primitive animal consciousness. It perverts man's animal nature to obstruct the natural processes of love.

As we all live in a violent world, on land that has been wrested by violence from whatever its former inhabitants, the Lords of the World have had to answer in strict terms this human question: "How can we take a youth, sweet-smelling and clean-skinned, out of his girl's arms, and train him so that on command he will infallibly do what we ask, though he die for it?"

This is the gist of the answer given in the war manuals:

Teach him to walk in measured steps. Teach him to chant in strict meter. Make him afraid of another man whose insignia designates him as superior. Teach him to obey. Teach him to obey regardless of sense or animal safety. Teach him to say, "Yes, sir!" Teach him to reply by rote. Teach him to turn his corners squarely. Teach him not to consider the meaning of the act, but to act out the command. Teach him that heaven is the name of a place with guarded streets where uniformed men march keeping order.

The Marine Corps manual is one of the great books. It tells: "How to creep: your body is kept free of the ground with your weight resting on forearms and lower legs. Your rifle is cradled in your arms to keep the muzzle out of dirt. . . . How to crawl. . . ."

It says: "Get the blade into the enemy. . . . Be ruthless, vicious, and fast in your attack. . . . The throat is the best target. The belly is good too . . . go for his hands, face, or sides with a hacking, slashing blade and cut your way to that vital area. . . . You must kill, not simply defeat your opponent. . . ."

Another greatness of the Marine Corps manual is that it lays bare the most vulnerable places, where neither art, nor the Holy Teachings, nor the processes of evolution have proven therapy to the sick beast in us.

In rehearsing *The Brig* we decided to use *The Guidebook* as our text.

My first reading of *The Brig* was a physical experience of the sense of total restriction. The restriction of the author to the barest facts, like the restrictions on the lives of the prisoners, immediately communicated the immobility of the structure. But what can be done within these strict limits? There is no alternate movement, no choice as to what shall be played upstage or downstage. No clue to the range of possible dramatic action. This is the key. The immobility of the structure. "Read the script," cries Piscator again and again in rehearsals. "Read the script."

The sparseness of human activity is demonstrated by the prisoner's day. It is the minimal man, confined to needs. He rises, washes, cleans his quarters, urinates, eats, smokes, is searched, works, eats, is frisked, works or cleans his quarters thoroughly, eats, writes a letter, showers, shaves, and sleeps. He also leaves the Brig, enters the Brig, flips out, marches, and has the living daylights beaten out of him. It isn't much. But where there is very little each action carries a greater burden of a man's suffering, as well as greater inklings of his smothered glory.

I understood this sparseness to be the "blind force" which "activates what it must activate" (i.e., the subservience of the man to the structure), which Artaud bids me explore when he says of the director:

The director, having become a kind of demiurge at the back of whose head is this idea of implacable purity and its consummation whatever the cost, if he truly wants to be a director, i.e., a man versed in the nature of matter and objects, must conduct in the physical domain an exploration of intense movement and precise emotional gesture, which is equivalent on the psychological level to the unchaining of certain blind forces which activate what they must activate and crush and burn on their way what they must crush and burn.

The question is, according to Artaud, where to begin the exploration of the movement and gesture equivalent to the psychological forces which activate *The Brig*?

For the answer I went to *The Guidebook,* which says, "Drill."

Drill inspires an individual to be a member of a team. The purposes of Drill are . . . to teach discipline by instilling habits of precision and automatic response to orders . . . to better morale.

And further it says:

Discipline is necessary to secure orderly action which alone can triumph over the seemingly impossible conditions of battle. . . . There is no sane person who is without fear, but with good discipline and high morale all can face danger.

Every situation has its own special problems and one of the problems particular to rehearsing *The Brig* at The Living Theatre was that atmosphere of permissiveness and informality which our working conditions have always favored. We are purposefully personal in the hope that the best work will generate within the greatest possible human warmth. We know that the price of discipline is the rigor of authority, the wages of order is submission. We know that the only real call to order is the needs of the work of art. Any other authority is usurped.

Now apply the strictest methods within the freest association. Reduce discipline to its lowest form (i.e., most harmless) as a spectacle to be observed as though it were rare. *As though it were rare!* Practice authority as though it were rare. At first I doubted that it would be possible for the company to make this unusual sacrifice and work in a manner opposed to the manner that has been developed as our social and artistic standard, that is, to formalize our relationship.

The formal relation is an immovable structure. Like all immovable structures it is the villain. We were going to set up villainy in a safe boundary as a biologist might use a Petri dish to grow a foul and noxious growth within a safe situation. We isolated it.

I prepare a play more by steeping myself in its mysteries

than by preparing a set of specific stage directions. I try to keep the action fluid for the actor, I like to reserve space in which the actor can move after that point in rehearsals when *he* knows more about the role than I did when we began. Therefore, I do not like to preset.

I prepared a set of "Rehearsal Regulations" which followed the form of the "Brig Regulations" that circumscribe the prisoners' action in the Brig. These "Brig Regulations" invented by the U.S. Marines are so basic to the action that we decided at the very beginning to print them in each program so that the spectator has the basic stage directions of *The Brig* in his hands.

These rehearsal rules imposed no requirements on the actor that the ordinary customs of the theatre do not demand of him, such as promptness, proper dress, silence. In the same way, the "Brig Regulations" are only the rules of military discipline imposed with cruelly demanding perfectionism. The free and easy spirit among us had to be transformed by sacrifice of our intimacy (just for the time of rehearsal) to the cold, hard way of the world. The rehearsal breaks and later the intermissions, where we resumed our friendly natures, would become paradisiacal interludes of life in the cold Brig world. The "Rehearsal Discipline" was presented to the company on mimeographed sheets before the first rehearsal. We were assembled on the stage in our usual, informal manner. We had been smoking and talking in the dressing rooms and our spirits were high with the excitement of rehearsing a new work with a familiar and trusted company. I explained that these rules would not be put into effect if any one person in the company did not wish to submit to any part of them.

They were written in the crass, effective, blunt style of the Marine Corps Brig Regulations. Here they are:

The Brig REHEARSAL DISCIPLINE

Because of the nature of the play, in which we are enacting a rigid discipline and demonstrating the results of an authoritarian environment, rehearsals will require a more than usual strict discipline. All members of the cast and crew are expected to be thoroughly familiar with the rules of this discipline, and, upon acceptance of the discipline by the entire company, are considered to be in agreement that they will work under these conditions.

1. *Rehearsal Time:* Rehearsal Time will be called by the stage manager at the beginning of every rehearsal period and at the end of every break period. During Rehearsal Time, all rules are in effect; during Break Time, rules are suspended. Break Time will be called by the stage manager, and will also be posted in advance—on the rehearsal board. In the event of a discrepancy between the posted time and the stage manager's call, the stage manager's call is to be the final word. At the start of each Rehearsal Time every actor is expected to be ready, in the auditorium, in proper clothing, for the call of places.

2. *Rehearsal Discipline Rules*

a. Actors will sign in before Rehearsal Time is called. Actors should arrive five minutes prior to called time, in the auditorium, to be ready for places when called.

b. During Rehearsal Time, actors who are not on stage will remain in the auditorium, ready to be called unless specifically dismissed by the stage manager.

c. During Rehearsal Time, there is to be no business or discussion other than that relating to the rehearsal.

d. No eating during Rehearsal Time.

e. Actors not required onstage may smoke in the first rows of the auditorium, where ash trays will be provided. No smoking in other parts of the auditorium. Backstage rules will be posted by the stage manager.

3. *Break Time:* During Break Time actors may leave the auditorium and the backstage area, but will not leave the building without informing the stage manager. (This rule not in effect during lunch and dinner breaks.) During breaks, actors are free to do whatever they please; all food, refuse,

and personal belongings must be cleared away *before* Rehearsal Time is called.

4. *Clothing:* Costumes will be issued as soon as possible; rehearsals will be in costume. Prior to costume rehearsal, actors will rehearse in clothes as follows: a T-shirt or light sweater, dungarees or work pants, a jockstrap, boxer shorts or bathing trunks, belts, heavy shoes (preferably high-top for prisoners), a zipper jacket (zelon-type), and a cap. Actors who cannot supply these items themselves will be outfitted by the stage manager. Make your application, for those items you cannot supply yourself, to the stage manager immediately. No extraneous jewelry or clothing will be worn during rehearsals or performance.

5. *Formality:* So that we may fully achieve the author's intent, the tone and atmosphere of Rehearsal Time will have to be more serious and formal than is usual. During Rehearsal Time, all actors and crew will maintain a respectful and serious attitude toward one another. There will be no joking tolerated during Rehearsal Time, especially in reference to the relationships of guards and prisoners.

6. *Penalties for infraction of rules:* The imposition of penalties is with the agreement, herewith, of the entire company. Penalties may be ordered by the director, the assistant director, the stage manager, the technical director. Penalties may be arbitrated, if the actor or crew member feels the penalty is unjust or uncalled for. Final decision rests with the producer. Penalties will all consist of work other than one's assigned work on the play. Work will be performed at any time the company member is not required in the course of his regular duties, during the rehearsal period and for the run, at times agreeable to the actor and stage manager and technical director, within a week.

7. *Tenative list of penalties* (to be finalized with company agreement at end of first week) :

Lateness: Doubletime work for time lost.

Absence: Singletime work for time lost. Lateness of more than four hours is considered absence.

Misconduct: (Obstructive, unco-operative behavior, such as kidding around on stage, unnecessary talks, failure to follow direction)—15 minutes work for each breach of discipline.

Failure to pass clothing inspection: (The stage manager will make a uniform inspection at the beginning of each Rehearsal Period, and gig those whose clothing is not in accordance with instructions; actors are responsible for all details of uniforms, including buttons)—15 minutes work time for each gig.

Loss of clothing: 1 hour work time per one dollar of clothing cost.

Loss of handprops: Same as above.

Additional penalties will be listed on the stage manager's backstage rules.

Additional rehearsal penalties will be posted if further discipline problems arise, but not without the agreement of the Company.

We talked for a long time about the gig system, and about the meaning of punishment. I feared the first ruffle of feelings. The actors agreed that a breach on their part would entail a penalty. No one dissented. To relieve the inevitable tensions we also instituted a five-minute break period which *any* actor could call at *any* time that he felt in need of freedom from the tensions and formality. Breaks were often called. They were never abused. We adjusted one clause in the fifth paragraph. Then the stage manager called rehearsal time.

Ash trays were set in the first two rows and the actors moved silently to their places for the first call. The silence was new to us. In it we felt the terrible loneliness of separation from one another. The lack of our usual laughter dismayed us. But we were thrilled by the silence and the formal tone and seeing our friends' faces so somber.

We used the techniques of evil as the innoculist uses the fatal virus. We absorbed it and we survived. We drilled. We exercised. We paid attention to accuracy. Ken Brown demonstrated for us how to slap the cap, how to make up the racks, how to swab, how to frisk and be frisked, in which hand to hold soap and toothbrush, the angle at which the manual is held; in fact, no detail was too insignificant for us to examine it for its physical appearance and its metaphysical equivalent.

This is what Artaud sought when he spoke of ritualizing objects.

There were some among us who remembered the Marine Corps from the inside and we questioned them for hours about the slightest aspect of that life that might prove useful. We sat around the dressing rooms long after rehearsal hours while Tom Lillard, who played the role of Prisoner Number Two, the figure of the author in *The Brig*, described to us the brig in which *he* served time, how it differed, how it was the same, how the soul got twisted and the body trained.

And as we worked in a new way we felt the hardness of the world outside, against which we had protected one another so long. We were like fleeing people who, even as they barricade themselves against the plague outside, meet the Red Death in their own fortified palace. But we knew that we were enacting him and the sting of his force was ritualistic fear. This power of ritual fear began to overwhelm the actors.

"If the blow does not hurt, why do I fear the white line?" Each one came to me to tell me of his own experience and they gathered together to talk each one of his terror of playing *The Brig*. The ordeal swept over us. We were all afraid. In the breaks we came closer and closer as we huddled together in small groups describing to each other the intricacies of this serious endeavor.

Moving with unaccustomed solemnity we learned to share the sense of the ordeal that the Marines felt at Fuji Brig, and that is everywhere felt in the schools of submission, in the fraternities of exclusion, in the clubs of the oppressors.

Drill was taught according to Marine Corps tactics. Chic Ciccarelli, who played the Brig Warden, was a former Marine, and remembered with touching and terrible closeness the cold, hard exhilaration of the drill. Before each rehearsal the company drilled half an hour, after the lunch break, another half hour. We cleared the lobby of The Living Theatre, and there on the tile floors we marched endless hours. Startled ticket buyers often entered in the middle of a drill master's angry scolding. It was not the polite tone of a theatrical director discussing the character with the actor, it was Ciccarelli screaming, "Get your head up, you lousy maggot!"

The drill however had an enlivening effect. The marching is a ritual of great beauty only grown hideous because it stands for the marches towards the fields of death in battle and because it has come to signify the loss of character that ensues when all of life becomes routed into this exactitude. And because you cannot stop. Meanwhile the rhythm of mutuality entices the kinetic senses. The sense of moving in a mutual rhythm with one's fellow man.

I had imagined marchers earlier, moving around the ritual circle in enormous savage costumes, when I saw the tribes of Dahomey dance their war dances on the stage of the Sarah Bernhardt Theatre in Paris. There was a time when they left those circles to move toward their enemies on what they called in the olden times the War Path. These marches, and the rhythm of the feet stamping on the hard path that time has cut through the ancient forests, were learned in the squares at the center of the villages. They were practiced in the threshing places, they were danced there in the theatres, and they took men to war in high spirits. The marching, they say, is a rest in a difficult routine.

After establishing the drill session and reading twice through the play we began to study the physical traits we would need. ("To know in advance what points of the body to touch is the key to throwing the spectator into magical trances." A.A.) And so we sought in each action its counterpart, its double in the human spirit.

Let us take for example those blows to the stomach that are such crucial moments in the play. The performer is transformed by them into a new kind of device for communication. This is known in athletics and circuses. I am talking about the imitative reflex action.

When the first blow is delivered in the darkened Brig before dawn and the prisoner winces and topples from his superbly rigid attention position, the contraction of his body is repeated *inside* the body of the spectator. That is, if we succeed, there is an actual physical, measurable contraction inside the spectator's body. We can at best be only partially successful in this. We ask for no more.

This instant of physical trauma is the instant in which a man becomes vulnerable. The human mind, vainly stabbing with the rigid prods of its will, cannot inhibit the softness of the soul as it asks for mercy for the body. The gentler spirit emerges for a moment in the red flash of brightness that accompanies the pang of a blow and pleads with the man (the whole man) to do whatever it may be to spare the beloved body continued or protracted or repeated pain. The Marine calls it cowardice and straightens up to attention as soon as the pain ebbs enough for his conditioned will to regain total power over his physical being.

We discussed at length the various stages of the blow, each one with their counterpart for prisoner and for guard. They are four:

1. The Moment before Impact: The prisoner draws upon his will and musters it for use as before battle. That is, he *hardens* himself both muscularly and psychologically. The guard prepares to make the impact of his blow telling. That is, he is concerned with making it hurt, let us say of a certain blow, not maim. He must gauge the degree to which he will let loose and the degree to which he will restrain. Being imbued with the notion of the Tough Marine he prepares

to let himself hurt the prisoner as much as he dares. He hardens himself in his mind in preparation for the blow (I believe, however, that the idea of mercy is at such a moment not as far from the surface as the Marine Corps would have us believe), just as he tightens the muscles of his fist, his arms, his back, his torso, and his legs in order to deliver the blow.

2. The Moment of Impact: (There is a moment before this but it is too swift and mysterious to discuss here. It has to do with movement.) This is the moment in which the prisoner has lost his total rigidity because now he can save himself only with resiliency. But resiliency is a feminine (*ergo:* cowardly) attribute. It must be used swiftly and superficially as always when we practice negative attributes for the sake of expedience. This moment is therefore brief. But this moment is the vulnerable moment at its climax. The hairs' breadth transition between the moment of impact and the moment of recovery centers first in the will as the mind flicks back from its instant of unconsciousness. Then, through the mustering of strength, it centers in the muscles in the man's body as it returns to the rigid position which the man's will proscribes for it. This moment is a physical moment and its attributes are physical. We had to be certain that this moment fulfilled its therapeutic function. At this crucial moment we must make this pain not the useless pain that sickness brings, or the inflicted pain that tempts us to vengeance and the perpetuation of the long line of hatred that had brought us here. This is the cathartic pain. We staked ourselves on catharsis.

The prisoner, hurt, is vulnerable and tender. His look betrays the baby's scream of agony at its first breath.

The guard, having hurt, untenses. But he knows the danger of slackening too long, lest the victim respond, not with defeat, but with anger. He is on guard. The guard waits for the prisoner now and reads him with the glance of a snake. (Spectator: Pity and Terror!)

3. The Moment of Recovery: The prisoner now enacts the will taking over. The rigid system at war with the animal need conquers all. Because he is a Marine.

The guard watches this process with a certain amount of satisfaction. If this part of the action is not executed properly, the guard will hit the prisoner again. This is the squared-away moment, when the hope that sprung out of the animal feelings during the blow itself lies unfulfilled. It is the point of return to that same hell out of which we emerged for a moment of suffering in the Theatre of Cruelty. There is no despair in this for the prisoner, but a sense of achievement. Having been laid low, he has recovered, and having recovered, he has regained his manhood. "You're making me sick with your little-girl tricks," says the guard to the prisoner who does not return quickly enough to the attention position. When we see him thus defeated in his victory it is for us, the audience, to respond to his helplessness. If the Moment of Impact has made us feel viscerally, then the Moment of Recovery should move us to revolutionary action for our fallen brother.

4. The First Moment of the New Status Quo: Each blow is a total demolition, each recovery a total restructure. After the blow the prisoner stands erect and proud, having, if not overcome, at least survived. Even if it hurts him.

The guard, however, is still tensed for the untoward event; the guard always suspects that the prisoner may flip out and hit him, especially after the blow. The guard has to play it longer, because the blow has made him insecure. He is often cheerful afterward, but sometimes angry or glum.

The spectator returns to the world in which this blow, this visceral pain, exists. In prizefights both men fight, and sympathy gets lost in swiftly dealt vengeance. But this blow belongs to the martyrs, the soldiers, and the poor.

Each particular of the play was examined with care and we talked without limit until we were all agreed on the meanings of each element, as Kenneth described it, as I tried to balance it, as the actors began to absorb it.

The Trip

Each actor brought back travelogues of a trip that he took out into the long silent stretches. Sometimes with his uniform soaking wet, or during and after a bout with the guards, or staring at the wire that hypnotized him with its glittering lines, he stood still inside that stillness within which the physical stillness lies hidden, and in that narrow space, being so strictly confined, took wing into what Artaud calls that "enormous spiral that reveals one perspective after another." The actor felt (some familiarly, some for the first time in their lives) the other self, the one that Artaud calls the Double, take flight and soar into that other space where time is not, nor relation, nor anything, but sheer existence, undefined and undefinable, seeming absolute.

The body of the prisoner is totally captive. The soul of the prisoner is potentially totally free. The trip between these two points is the crucial experience of the play.

From this time forward the actor moves inside the Brig with mysterious immunity. "And behind the Warrior, is The Double . . . who, roused by the repercussion of the turmoil, moves unaware in the midst of spells of which he has understood nothing."

At first embarrassed confessions passed among close friends. Then some came to me for consultation, worried about this "symptom," while some shouted joyfully, "I made it." Each actor in his own way confronted the moment when the body submits to the other part, so indistinguishable from the body that all the forms of holiness never cease telling us that they are one. And they are one. These two, felt by the ego as independent, suffer by their separation. Suffering melds a man and his soul.

The action of *The Brig* is real, physical, here-and-now. The spirit needs force to fuse again with the athletic body, thus its strictures become the means for this sense of unification.

I asked the actors about the Trip. They said:

1. "The space traversed is infinite."
2. "You can't think further than the next white line."

The White Line

These plain white markings on the deck of the Brig represent the simplicity with which the torture is inflicted. They are the points designated by authority beyond which we may not go, and in that capacity are related to an ancient taboo, and one not without psychological and mythological analogies. Where have we met the uncrossable line before? What echo does it stir?

It stirs the recollection of that other untraversable line: the Magic Circle. The Magic Circle is drawn by the sorcerer around the victim who stands helpless within it while the spell is woven around him. The ancient authority and the new do not differ in this: the belief of the victim in the power of the Authority makes what is unreal real. It is because he believes himself thus trapped that he is thus trapped, and as the guards say in *The Brig*, "You *better* believe it!"

They are easily justified by those who painted them there. Why, they are merely lines for the regulation of traffic through congested areas, a convenience to keep passageways clear and control movement around the Brig. The preoccupation with cleanliness which makes it dangerous to step on and dirty the white line, or the preoccupation with exactitude (squared-awayness) which makes it punishable to step on a white line are special pathologies always associated with the fear of mutiny. The implications of the word "shipshape" are the captain's preventative against mutiny. The White Line is this and more than this.

In a great and pertinent book, called *Drawing the Line*, Paul Goodman tells us:

In the mixed society of coercion and nature, our characteristic act is Drawing the Line beyond which we cannot co-operate. All the heart-searching and purgatorial anxiety concerns this question, *Where to draw the line?* I'll say it bluntly: The anxiety goes far beyond reason. . . .

Yet to each person it seems to make all the difference where he draws the line! This is because *these details are the symbolic key to his repressed powers.*

The prisoners in the Brig draw the line at the line. Beyond that is pain. This line, "the Line beyond which we cannot co-operate," is drawn alike by prisoner and guard, and the suffering of the guard is our unremitting concern. Paul goes on:

A free man would have no such problems; he would not have finally to draw a line in their absurd conditions which he has disdained from the very beginning. . . .

No particular drawn line will ever be defensible logically. But the right way away from any line will prove itself more clearly step by step and blow by blow.

In every action where hate is the motive, we divulged the element which, however buried, twisted, racked, and punched it may be, is love, the saving grace in everything human. We called on pity last, on basic human kinship first.

Here are a dozen particulars, that marked our way:

1. How the relationship between the guard and the prisoner is the human cornerstone of the play. Where does the I-and-Thou get lost? "Why do they call them maggots?" I asked a cocky young Marine. "Lowest form of animal life," he answered with a cocky smile.

2. How the relationship of the prisoners toward one another is the hope of the world. One actor says: "Just as we knew where our fellow prisoner was standing and what he was doing without looking at him, so we came to know how he was feeling, if he was in pain, or if he was happy because he was clicked in. It was like telepathy. But it wasn't that. It was community."

3. How the guards come to be there and how they survived the horror of their ordeal. Ken told me they were chosen at random. Aptitude graded to be brig guards. They have two alternatives, but to fail to fulfill their assignment

is to fail as a Marine. *How They Learn to Love It* is the name of their tragic play.

4.   How the phrase "It's your night tonight" sets a man's head and body loose into a net of apprehension. The day-long fear is as bad as the beating. The theory of deterrence is the discipline of the Brig. (Ask: *Where* does it hurt?)

5.   How the author, in the opening scene, enters the character of Prisoner Number Two whose "night it is," and how at first we see the Brig through his staunch, frightened eyes, but later in the day he is immersed in the fraternity of not suffering alone; not knowing his fellow's name, he learns to live in silent empathy with him, till the author's ego and the actor's individuality and the audience's sense of personal uniqueness are swallowed up in the narrow strictures of the Brig's confining rules.

6.   How Prisoner Number Three has learned to exist in the darkness as if he were living in the light. "Why doesn't he get hit?" they ask. Because he has been there so long!

7.   How Prisoner Number Five gives us hope that there is a way out. That it ends, somehow. And not always too late. But what does he go to when he gets out the Freedom Door?

8.   How Prisoner Number Six gets back his name: he observes the ceremonial leave-taking of Five with horror. Then, *he disobeys the next command.* He doesn't move on the line "Get back to your manuals." He just stands there. The audience notices it before the guards do, and if we are doing it right they anticipate the scream. Before he screams he has disobeyed the command. He screams because he has broken out of the system. Because he has isolated himself forever. Because he cannot go back. He is afraid. And he is not afraid because he has gone crazy, but because he has gone sane.

"My name is not Six," he cries out, "it's James Turner. Let me out of here." As he flails about to escape the entrapping jacket, the guard says "Just relax, James Turner, you are getting out of here." This is the only instance in which a prisoner is referred to by his name. For an instant the prisoner is deluded that the minion of law and order has restored him to the status of a man. He relaxes, and this is the fatal moment when they bind him and carry him out on a stretcher, as he says "Thank God."

But *where* are they taking him? He has a rendezvous out there with an unknown, impenetrable, giant Brig called the Looney-Bin where tomorrow's hospital-prisons are already a-building on the ruins of the ancient dungeons. When the prison reformers have torn down the walls, the "sick criminal" will be incarcerated there among the antiseptic horrors of the shock-machines and the well-meaning psychiatric case-workers. What trap shall we be in then? Into what darkness shall we be swallowed?

9.   How the tears of Prisoner Number Eight remind everyone of something that happened long ago when pride lost out to feeling.

10.   How the roles of prisoners who have no special business are as total as the roles with speaking scenes because each actor played each prisoner with his own peculiar sensuality.

11.   How the second Prisoner Five perpetuates the process so that the structure will have no end. There is by now something pathetically weary and comical about the prisoner. As if he had been going on forever. The last tragedy. (Laughter/resignation.)

12.   How the field day becomes a bacchanal of terror and intoxication: beginning with the first requests to cross, the sound rises toward a "sonorous pulsation."

These overlapping sounds were of two kinds and their mystery of two kinds. This climax of the ritual of useless work and the wasting of manly strength, and the abuse of the beautiful by the strong, contains the two kinds of sounds which echo the diabolical resonances of life in and out of the Brig.

The sound of the work is clashing, disorganized, disordered, confused, tumultuous. It is irregular and violent. It differed in each performance. I urged the actors to listen to this sound, to strain to catch its modulations. They attended even in the midst of the physical exertion of the field day, their bodies sweating and breathless and tired. But their ears open. I asked them to hear it and respond to it. They built its roar each night differently, but always with an attentive ear to what was happening within all earshot. Their animal ears and instincts awake in the deafening dark. They built it to a steady crescendo, climaxing at the singing of the hymn when they softened it to let the poetry ring through the bellowing rhythms of their labors.

Then the marching in Post Two begins to dominate the scene. As each prisoner joins in the drill, the disordered sound abates. The reverberating rigid sound takes over. How pleasant the steady drone is after the wild clangor. The drill sounds are regular, organized, orderly, controlled, disciplined. They are regular and law abiding. The actors were troubled by how restful it was. They didn't want to be enfolded in its harmony, the reconciliation of its smooth, untroubled, monotonous comfort.

Every night that they made this music and did this dreadful pantomime they enacted what it came to:

The price of the chaos under which we suffer.

The price of the rigid law which gives us a slave's ease.

When the audience can know violence in the clear light of the kinship of our physical empathy, it will go out of the theatre and turn such evil into such good as transformed the Furies into the Kindly Ones.

If the audience sees violence only in the dark light of the TV horror Western it will go out of its house with its rifle under its arm.

Violence is the darkest place of all. Let us throw light on it. In that light we will confront the dimensions of the Structure, find its keystone, learn on what foundations it stands, and locate its doors. Then we will penetrate its locks and open the doors of all the jails.

JUDITH MALINA

New York City
July 1964

DRAMABOOKS

WHEN ORDERING, please use the Standard Book Number consisting of the publisher's prefix, 8090-, plus tne five digits following each title. (Note that the numbers given in this list are for paperback editions only. Many of the books are also available in cloth.)

MERMAID DRAMA BOOKS

Christopher Marlowe (Tamburlaine the Great, Parts I & II, Doctor Faustus, The Jew of Malta, Edward the Second) (0701–0)

William Congreve (Complete Plays) (0702–9)

Webster and Tourneur (The White Devil, The Duchess of Malfi, The Atheist's Tragedy, The Revenger's Tragedy) (0703–7)

John Ford (The Lover's Melancholy, 'Tis Pity She's a Whore, The Broken Heart, Love's Sacrifice, Perkin Warbeck) (0704–5)

Richard Brinsley Sheridan (The Rivals, St. Patrick's Day, The Duenna, A Trip to Scarborough, The Schoo¹ for Scandal, The Critic) (0705–3)

Camille and Other Plays (Scribe: A Peculiar Position, The Glass of Water; Sardou: A Scrap of Paper; Dumas: Camille; Augier: Olympe's Marriage) (0706–1)

John Dryden (The Conquest of Granada, Parts I & II, Marriage à la Mode, Aureng-Zebe) (0707–X)

Ben Jonson Vol. 1 (Volpone, Epicoene, The Alchemist) (0708–8)

Oliver Goldsmith (The Good Natur'd Man, She Stoops to Conquer, An Essay on the Theatre, A Register of Scotch Marriages) (0709–6)

Jean Anouilh Vol. 1 (Antigone, Eurydice, The Rehearsal, Romeo and Jeannette, The Ermine) (0710–X)

Let's Get a Divorce! and Other Plays (Labiche: A Trip Abroad, and Célimare; Sardou: Let's Get a Divorce!; Courteline: These Cornfields; Feydeau: Keep an Eye on Amélie; Prévert: A United Family; Achard: Essays on Feydeau) (0711–8)

Jean Giraudoux Vol. 1 (Ondine, The Enchanted, The Madwoman of Chaillot, The Apollo of Bellac) (0712–6)

Jean Anouilh Vol. 2 (Restless Heart, Time Remembered, Ardèle, Mademoiselle Colombe, The Lark) (0713–4)

Henrik Ibsen: The Last Plays (Little Eyolf, John Gabriel Borkman, When We Dead Awaken) (0714–2)

Ivan Turgenev (A Mouth in the Country, A Provincial Lady, A Poor Gentleman) (0715–0)

George Farquhar (The Constant Couple, The Twin-Rivals, The Recruiting Officer, The Beaux Stratagem) (0716–9)

Jean Racine (Andromache, Britannicus, Berenice, Phaedra, Athaliah) (0717–7)

The Storm and Other Russian Plays (The Storm, The Government Inspector, The Power of Darkness, Uncle Vanya, The Lower Depths) (0718–5)

Michel de Ghelderode: Seven Plays Vol. 1 (The Ostend Interviews, Chronicles of Hell, Barabbas, The Women at the Tomb, Pantagleize, The Blind Men, Three Players and a Play, Lord Halewyn) (0719–3)

Lope de Vega: Five Plays (Peribáñez, Fuenteovejuna, The Dog in the Manger, The Knight from Olmedo, Iustice Without Revenge) (0720–7)

Calderón: Four Plays (Secret Vengeance for Secret Insult, Devotion to the Cross, The Mayor of Zalamea, The Phantom Lady) (0721–5)

Jean Cocteau: Five Plays (Orphée, Antigone, Intimate Relations, The Holy Terrors, The Eagle with Two Heads) (0722–3)

Ben Jonson Vol. 2 (Every Man in His Humour, Sejanus, Bartholomew Fair) (0723–1)

Port-Royal and Other Plays (Claudel: Tobias and Sara; Mauriac: Asmodée; Copeau: The Poor Little Man; Montherlant: Port-Royal) (0724–X)

Edwardian Plays (Maugham· Loaves and Fishes; Hankin: The Return of the Prodigal; Shaw: Getting Married; Pinero: Mid-Channel; Granville-Barker: The Madras House) (0725–8)

Alfred de Musset: Seven Plays (0726–6)

Georg Büchner: Complete Plays and Prose (0727–4)

Paul Green: Five Plays (Johnny Johnson, In Abraham's Bosom, Hymn to the Rising Sun, The House of Connelly, White Dresses) (0728–2)

François Billetdoux: Two Plays (Tchin-Tchin, Chez Torpe) (0729–0)

Michel de Ghelderode: Seven Plays Vol. 2 (Red Magic, Hop, Signor!, The Death of Doctor Faust, Christopher Columbus, A Night of Pity, Piet Bouteille, Miss Jairus) (0730–4)

Jean Giraudoux Vol. 2 (Siegfried, Amphitryon 38, Electra) (0731–2)

Kelly's Eye and Other Plays by Henry Livings (Kelly's Eye, Big Soft Nellie, There's No Room for You Here for a Start) (0732–0)

Gabriel Marcel: Three Plays (Man of God, Ariadne, Votive Candle) (0733–9)

New American Plays Vol. 1, ed. by Robert W. Corrigan (0734–7)

Elmer Rice: Three Plays (Adding Machine, Street Scene, Dream Girl) (0735–5)

The Day the Whores Came Out to Play Tennis . . . by Arthur Kopit (0736–3)

Platonov by Anton Chekhov (0737–1)

Ugo Betti: Three Plays (The Inquiry, Goat Island, The Gambler) (0738–X)

Jean Anouilh Vol. 3 (Thieves' Carnival, Medea, Cécile, Traveler Without Luggage, Orchestra, Episode in the Life of an Author, Catch As Catch Can) (0739-8)

Max Frisch: Three Plays (Don Juan, The Great Rage of Philip Hotz, When the War Was Over) (0740-1)

New American Plays Vol. 2 ed. by William M. Hoffman (0741-X)

Plays from Black Africa ed. by Fredric M. Litto (0742-8)

Anton Chekhov: Four Plays (The Seagull, Uncle Vanya, The Cherry Orchard, The Three Sisters) (0743-6)

The Silver Foxes Are Dead and Other Plays by Jakov Lind (The Silver Foxes Are Dead, Anna Laub, Hunger, Fear) (0744-4)

THE NEW MERMAIDS

Bussy D'Ambois by George Chapman (1101-8)
The Broken Heart by John Ford (1102-6)
The Duchess of Malfi by John Webster (1103-4)
Doctor Faustus by Christopher Marlowe (1104-2)
The Alchemist by Ben Jonson (1105-0)
The Jew of Malta by Christopher Marlowe (1106-9)
The Revenger's Tragedy by Cyril Tourneur (1107-7)
A Game at Chess by Thomas Middleton (1108-5)
Every Man in His Humour by Ben Jonson (1109-3)
The White Devil by John Webster (1110-7)
Edward the Second by Christopher Marlowe (1111-5)
The Malcontent by John Marston (1112-3)
'Tis Pity She's a Whore by John Ford (1113-1)
Sejanus His Fall by Ben Jonson (1114-X)

SPOTLIGHT DRAMABOOKS

The Last Days of Lincoln by Mark Van Doren (1201-4)
Oh Dad, Poor Dad . . . by Arthur Kopit (1202-2)
The Chinese Wall by Max Frisch (1203-0)
Billy Budd by Louis O. Coxe and Robert Chapman (1204-9)
The Devils by John Whiting (1205-7)
The Firebugs by Max Frisch (1206-5)
Andorra by Max Frisch (1207-3)
Balm in Gilead and Other Plays by Lanford Wilson (1208-1)
Matty and the Moron and Madonna by Herbert Lieberman (1209-X)
The Brig by Kenneth H. Brown (1210-3)
The Cavern by Jean Anouilh (1211-1)
Saved by Edward Bond (1212-X)
Eh? by Henry Livings (1213-8)
The Rimers of Eldritch and Other Plays by Lanford Wilson (1214-6)
In the Matter of J. Robert Oppenheimer by Heinar Kipphardt (1215-4)
Ergo by Jakov Lind (1216-2)
Biography: A Game by Max Frisch (1217-0)

For a complete list of books of criticism and history of the drama, please write to Hill and Wang, 72 Fifth Avenue, New York, New York 10011.